A Friend Indeed

SRI SRI GOURA GADADHAROU VIJAYETAM

A Friend Indeed

(Sri Gadadhara Pundit the real friend of Sri Gouranga)

Radhakrishana Goswami

ISBN: 978-93-5324-965-6

First Published, 2022

Published by

Kalpaz Publications
C-30, Satyawati Nagar,
Delhi – 110052
Ph.: 011-47034999, 9811692060
www.kalpazpublications.com
E-mail: kalpaz@hotmail.com

Printed at: Gyan Press, Delhi.

The Author is much happy to dedicate the Book

To

Affectionate

Shri Dipankar Ghosh, M.A., B-Ed., M.Phil., PhD.

With Goodwishes

Contents

Author's Note 11

I. Sri Gouranga 15

Vasudhaiva Kutumbakam 15
Sripad Madhabendrapuri 15
Sri Gouranga's Belief 16
Sri Vishwarup and Nemai 18
Childhood of Nemai 19
Hindolika Riding with Gadadhar 23
Reality for Family Life 26
Laxmipriya Devi 26
Vidyavilas by Sri Gouranga 28
Sri Gadadhara Pundit 31
Sri Keshav Kashmiri Pundit 33
Nemai in East Bengal (now in Bangladesh) 38
Nemai's Marriage with Vishnupriyadevi 39
Nemai with Gadadhara met People of different Occupations 40

II. Harinaam Sankirtan Mahayajna 41

Ishwarpuri in disguise arrived at Nabadwip 41
Nemai at Gaya and Initiation from Ishwarpuri 42
Shyamang Hiranyaparidhing... 44
Sri Gouranga's Madness Enhanced 45
Sri Gouranga's Planning 47
Harinaam Sankirtan 47
Sri Gouranga-Gadadhara at Sri Adwaita Acharya 48
Harinaam Sankirtan Movement Geared up 50
Haridas 52
Inclusion of Sri Nityanandaprabhu as Abadhoot 53
Pundarik Vidyanidhi and Sri Gadadhara's Initiation 54
Engrossment of Lord Nrisinha 59
Engrossment of Lord Shiva Mahadeva 61
Jagai and Madhai became Vaishnava 61
'Bhagawatacharya's Initiation- Sri Gadadhara Pundit 64

III. Harinaam Sankirtan got Maturity **67**
Laxmi Kaachh or Rukmini Sambad - Drama 67
Harinaam Continues 71
Brahmin-curse as a Boon 72
An Intruder Brahmin 72
Mother-in-law of Sribaas 72
Narayani a Female Child and Sri Vrindabandas 72
'Dukhi' to 'Sukhi' 73
Chapal Gopal 74
Worshipping of Lord Vishnu by Sri Gouranga 75
At the house of Shuklambar Brahmachari 75
Murari Gupta 76
The Mahamantra Harinaam 78
Kazi Vijay 78
A Sad Incidence 84
Kripa of Srimati Radharani 85
Again on the Street of Nabadwip 86
Sannyas 87
Sri Adwaita Acharya at Shantipur 93

IV. On Way to Neelachal **95**
From Shantipur 95
At Atisara 95
At Chhatrabhog 95
Service of Ramchandra Khan 95
At Prayag Ghat 96
Nityananda Broke the Stick 97
At Remuna 98
At Jajpur 100
Shakshi Gopal at Cuttack 100
At Bhubaneswar 100
At Kamalpur 101
At Atharonala 101

V. Neelachal Leela 1 .... **103**
"Jagannathaswami Nayana Pathagami Bhabatu Me... 103
Sri Sarbabhoum 104
Sri Chaitanyadeva Discovered the Deity of Gopinath 105
Tour in South India 106

VI. Neelachal Leela 2 .... **111**
King Pratap Rudra wanted to Meet Sri Chaitanyadeva 111

Swarup Damodar Joined Sri Chaitanyadeva 113
Paramananda Puri's Well 113
Desire to Travel Vrindaban via Goud Banga 114
Sri Chaitanyadeva returned to Neelachal 122
Raghav's Jhali 123
Gundicha Margan 123
Rathayatragre Sri Chaitanyadeva 124
Goudiya Vaishnavas in Neelachal 132
Followers in Odisha 134

VII. Travel to Mathura-Vrindaban 135
Walking through the Forest of Jharikhand 135
Sri Roop 138
Sri Sanatan 140
Return from Mathura-Vrindaban at Narendra Sarobar in Puri 143
Ballav Bhatta in Puri 143
Correction of Diksha Mantra of Gadadhara Pundit 145
Sri Raghunath Das Goswami 146

VIII. The Rathayatra 151
Goudiya Vaishnavas in Neelachal 2nd Time 151
Bakreswar Pundit 152
Sri Gopal Guru 152
Goudiya Vaishnavas in Neelachal 3rd Time 153
Teachings by Lifestyle 154
Not to Cross Limit 155
No Pain Physically or Mentally to Others 155
Due Respect to Women 156
Hard Reality and Sri Chaitanyadev 157
The Last Twelve Years of Sri Chaitanyadev 158

***Appendices* 163**

***Index* 173**

Author's Note

The very caption Sri Sri Goura Gadadhara Vijayetam on the top of the heading was originally used by Sri Roop Goswami in Vrindaban in his authored books.

A few years back after my retirement in 2006, I have commenced to read some valuable books and simultaneously was working on the lives of Sri Chaitanyadeva and his associates like Sri Gadadhara Pundit, Sri Nityanandaprabhu, Sri Adwaita Acharya, Sri Sribaas, Sri Haridas and others. Somehow, I became interested about the divine lives of them specially, Sri Chaitanyadeva and Sri Gadadhara Pundit as the latter had insufficient mentions in the books written in earlier times.

On knowing my interest in writing on Sri Chaitanyadeva and Sri Gadadhara some of my retired colleagues who had hardly knowledge with Goud Bengal's Vaishnava Movement except the name of Sri Chaitanyadeva asked me with enthusiasm - "Are you writing about our Sri Ramkrishna whose original name was Gadadhara?"

I humbly replied to them - "No, Gadadhar or Sri Ramkrishna was born in 1836 AD at Kamarpukur while this Gadadhara was born in 1486 AD just after one month and a half years later of holy birth of Sri Gouranga Mahaprabhu or Sri Chaitanyadeva. So, there remains 350 years' gap of the births of them."

Once certain Professor of Bengali also asked me - "Was it Gadadhara Das?"

I again humbly answered - "No Sir, you are talking about junior Gadadhara and who was named as Das Gadadhara. The subject of my Gadadhara is called by the Vaishnavas as Gadadhara Pundit who always remained to be with Sri Gouranga Mahaprabhu or Sri Chaitanyadeva."

To the revered readers, I like to introduce you with Sri Gadadhara Pundit who sacrificed everything earthly only to serve unconditionally to his friend Sri Gouranga or Sri Chaitanyadeva. Sri Gadadhara Pundit was so important that once many of the devotees of Bengal and Odisha also began to worship the combined deities of Sri Gouranga and Sri Gadadhara Pundit.

(Samsad Bangali Charitavidhan, 1st Part, p. 128, Pub. Sahitya Samsad)

We can cite that once the eminent composer Sri Basudeva Ghose sang the beauty of this divine deity of Goura-Gadadhara (combined two). He had prayed that his desire to serve Goura-Gadadhara births after births could be fulfilled.

The emotions for Sri Gouranga and expression of Pundit Sri Gadadhara are not possible to describe in languages. Sri Gouranga can be termed as the "Lord of the life of Sri Gadadhara". Their glories are sung by also some of the devotees as Gadai-Gouranga.

Moreover, Sri Gadadhara Pundit, the lifelong company remained unmarried only for rendering unconditional services to Lord Sri Krishna and his Lord Sri Gouranga.

Sri Gadadhara Pundit and Sri Gouranga always remained closedly with each other. Their friendship began from their childhood as their mothers used to meet each other with their sons in the laps almost everyday.

The revered readers, such a lifelong associate of Sri Chaitanyadeva should not be ignored or a little mention as we find almost in the literature.

So I, a tiny writer, took up the pen (here a mouse of Computer) in hand in order to draw a sketch a friend Sri Gadadhara Pundit in need is a friend indeed to Sri Gouranga Mahaprabhu.

It is known the facts and figures given here all may not match with the life of only Sri Gadadhara Pundit. So, in love to Sri Gouranga (Sri Chaitanyadeva) many of the incidents were discussed in it where the activities of Sri Gadadhara Pundit were not found.

However, the author is confident that without the happenings of Sri Chaitanyadeva no one character of his associates could be completed. For the writing of the life of any of the associates the happenings in the life of Sri Chaitanyadeva should be added, otherwise the aim of the write up would not show a complete picture.

Being completely confined at house during the present uncommon Pandemic situation, while I at my 75 was preparing the manuscript my wife Smt. Bhumika Goswami who is also a write, narrator of Srimad

Bhagawata Geeta 'Sri Mad Bhagawata asked me why I was doing the job of writing on the subject Sri Gadadhara Pundit again?' I replied - "Yes, in Bengali and English books like 'Sri Chaitanyadev and Gadadhar' and 'Sri Nityananda with Gouranga Gadadhar' etc. have already been published but this book differs from those. It has a different angle." However, she co-operated me, otherwise, I could not prepare it.

Must I am to offer my gratitude to Mr. Amit Garg MD of Kalpaz Publications as well as Gyan Printers. I also fell indebtedness to the people who composed this work, the Proof readings, the binding workers and the people who run the office of the Publishers. Thank you all.

I hope, this writing in broken and ordinary English would give you the exact conception about Sri Gadadhara Pundit and also other associates of and including Sri Chaitanyadeva. - Author.

I. Sri Gouranga

Vasudhaiva Kutumbakam

We should know that, "Nothing human is alien to us. We are no more members of this or that particular group belong to humanity as a whole". Again, "In fact, today what needs is not much more Hiduism but its glowing vision of mankind as a family Vasudhaiva Kutumbakam.

(Religion and Society and South Eastern Religions and Western Thoughts by Dr. S. Radhakrishnan)

Vaishnavism welcomes everyone of this earth. The thoughts were on social lives and religious simplicity that attracted even to the mere illiterate people almost living below the poverty line. The socially deprived of human prestige for ordinary people was thought by Vaishnavism first and thereafter they have got the opportunity to breathe on this earth easily. God, the supreme creator has created all the Jibas including human beings. He, who knows should consider others as his relatives because the almighty God, in whatever name you call Him, lives in every creature of the Universe. This is called Love. Love without enemity. In the world now full of poison the need of love is the most essential. Sri Chaitanyadeva was the incarnation of Love, love to God Lord Sri Krishna and love to all the creations of the Universe.

Sripad Madhabendrapuri

Almost six centuries back India got a pioneer preacher of Lord Sri Krishna's Love i.e. Love for the Universe. With this mission once Sripad Madhabendrapuri by having roamed at different pilgrims reached Nabadwip what was inhabitated by hundreds of scholars, teachers, students and devotees of Lord Krishna. He traveled many houses of his disciples there. He had a good number of capable disciples with whom he succeded to sow the seed of Harinaam among many common people. They were Paramananda Puri, Sri Rangapuri, Pundarik Vidyanidhi (preceptor of Gadadhar Pundit), Sri Adwaitacharya, Brahmanandapuri, Brahmananda Bharti, Maithil Vishnupuri, Raghupati Upadhyay, Karishnananda, Nrisingha

Tirtha, Sukhanandapuri, Ramchandrapuri,Raghunathpuri, Ananatapuri, Gopalpuri, Sankarshan Puri, Jagannath Mishra, Ratnagarva Acharya, Suklambar Brahmachari, Gangadas Pundit, Hiranya Pundit, other pundits like Sadshiva, Jagadish, SriBaas, Madhab Mishra (Father of Gadadhar Pundit), Ishwarpuri (first preceptor of Lord Gouranga) and many others from different corners of India.

Sripad Madhabendrapuri was born in almost six hundred years back in the district of Sylhet (Srihatta) in East Bengal in a Barendra Brahmin family of Kashyapa Gotra. It is learnt that his ancestor Swarnarekh received a village named Karja in Barendrabhumi area from the then Emperor of Pal dynasty Dharmapal.

In his early stage he a devotee of Sri Krishna became a learned professor and eminent among his students in East Bengal. After giving birth to a son, his wife all of a sudden succumbed. Afterwards he with the child came to Vishnupur village in between Kulia and Kumarhatta in the district of North 24 Parganas West Bengal and settled a school there. Here once came young Ishwarpuri to learn Scriptures and the Religion of Love. Here another young person from Laur Pargana of Srihatta Kamalakshya Bhattacharya, later widely known as Sri Adwaitacharya, came and started to learn Scriptures and Religion of Love for God.

It is also learnt that Sripad Madhabendrapuri visited Nabadwip in 1411 Saka. On the 6th birthday of Nemai he was present at the house of Sri Jagannath Mishra and was surprised to note some special signs in the five years' boy. He also found the beautiful Gadadhara the youngest son of Madhab Mishra. He offered good wishes to Nemai and Gadadhara. He was fully contended that in future this boy with his company and others would be able to quench the thirsts of millions of devotees who would know nothing but Lord Sri Krishna. In the next year Madhabendrapuri breathed his last at Remuna near the Temple of Khirchora Gopinath.

We understand Sripad Madhabendrapuri was satisfied to see little Neemai that his dream of Harinaam Movement would be successful with this little boy's efforts in near future.

Sri Gouranga's Belief

First, a Man of Reality was Sri Gouranga. He was also a matured personality with vast knowledge in literature, rhetoric, grammar, logic, philosophy etc. and in many subjects and above all in scriptures of various philosophies. So, undoubtedly we can comment 'a Man of Reality was Sri

Gouranga'. In ecstasy He became mad off and on. It was devotion, belief and sincerity for normal love for God, in whatever name He was called.

But on this earth the reality cannot be counted with only the religious practices observed in a human being. A real human of this earth can be judged depending on his activities, practices and beliefs. One should be termed as a man if he possesses the quality of humanity. Sri Gouranga was a man and a man of reality. He had soft corners for the people surroundings and also in other countries. He had also love-affection for the ordinary people and so, he had occasionally been at the houses of different occupations.

He found that in the society there remain disorder, envy, enmity, cruelty, lack of showing respect to seniors and others. He also noticed inhumanic torture, hatred and insulting the people who live on their laborious jobs in the fields of harvesting food grains, green vegetables, fishing in the rivers and seas and working in small and big factories etc. He also observed torture on the people on whose labour the elite people could live on. He had seen uncultured behave and lacking in spreading education in the society.

He knew there is one and only one God from whose desire the people and all Jibas and the Universe were created or born. So, he once wrote:-

Naamnamkari Bahudha Nija Sarba Shakti Satatraarpita,
Etadrishi Taba Kripa Bhaganamapi
Durdoibamidrishajoni Naanuragah.

(No. 2 of Shiksha Sloakastaka
by Sri Chaitanayadeva)

Naamnakari Bahudha - He has kindly exposed Himself in many names. He has rest all His power on those Names too.

People have the beliefs in that Naam and Naami (bearer of the name) are the same and identical and also important. By memorising Lord to utter His name there is not necessary to obey any rules. Sri Chaitanyadeva urged by saying - Oh! Lord, such Your kindness is as you remain. But alas, my misfortune is that I have no attachment in thy name (whatever according to different beliefs different names You possess).

Sri Vishwarup and Nemai

Nemai or Sri Gouranga or Sri Chaitanyadeva had only one elder brother Vishwaroop. He was also looked like a saint from his very childhood. He was also a serious student of Sri Adwaita Acharya. Often he would pass whole of the day by discussing on the Gita, the Upanishads, the Vedas with Sri Adwaita Acharya. His parents while were arranging to get their elder son married he thought to himself not to be tied in 'Maya' i.e. family bondage and so he left home for ever. It was heard that he took Sannyas in search of God. Later he was named as Shankaranya as a Sannyasi.

One day Sri Adwaita Acharya was engaged in teaching the Vedanta and their narrations to his students in the 'Tole' in Nabadwip. Amongst the students meritorious Vishwaroop was receiving lessons from him. It was almost the time of lunch but Vishwaroop was so involved on lesson that neither he nor his teacher could be conscious about the time. Sachimaa was anxious for her elder son. Without him she could not take meal. She thought that after bathing in the Ganga very early in the morning Vishwaroop used to meet Adwyaitacharya to discuss different topics of the old Scriptures. Vishwaroop preferred to remain with Sri Adwyaitacharya all the time. Her Vishwaroop, however, after bathing took breakfast and went for learning the Vedas and the Upanishads to Sri Adwaita Acharya. The breakfast, as usally, was of little amount. Perhaps he was much hungry now. So, she called the younger Nemai who was playing with clays. Nemai nearer to 5/6 years' old boy was almost without dress, as the then usual customs at home only.

Sri Adwyaitacharya's Nabadwip residence with the Tole was not far. Sachimaa called - "Nemai, Nemai please call your elder brother back to take lunch. Please make haste".

Neither she nor little Nemai cared for any proper dress as the 'Tole' was nearer. Nemai being advised by mother without wasting any moment ran towards the 'Tole' the house of Sri Adwyaitacharya without caring for own dress.

From outside the 'Tole' he shouted - "Dada, Dada. Maa is waiting for you. Your lunch is being cold. Come sharp."

At that time of Sri Adwyaitacharya was discussing the Vedas and the Upanishads with Vishwaroop and other students. He affectionately looked at and was highly satisfied with the divine, appearance Nemai had.

Prati ange nirupam labonyer seema
Koti Chandra nah eek nekher upama.
Digambar sarva anga dhulay dhusar
Haasiya agraja prati karaye uttar.

(Sri Chaitanya Bhagawat 1/6
by Vrindavandas)

He remained looking without any blink of eyes for a long time. Here Sri Adwaitacharya got the chance to look little Nemai on whose body all the symptoms of a great personality or God were present. He also observed many uncommon signs in dressless child Nemai. He understood that his dream and longdrawn prayer to Lord Sri Krishna's coming at last going to be successful in near future.

Sri Adwaitaacharya from the portico saw him when Nemai came there to call Vishwaroop. Sri Adwyaitacharya availed the opportunity of seeing little Nemai and listened to the call but could not speak a single word. He was just remained looking at the child Nemai of 5 to 6 years' old. He observed the full body of Nemai and was astonished to find the signs all over the body were of a man of supernatural powers with lot of possibilities of becoming a man of the men. Then he thought it might be fortune for the people that God has incarnated Himself.

On the other hand, Vishwaroop had great affection for his brother Nemai. He had anxiety for the younger brother as observed naughtiness at the Ghats of the Ganga. Sometime Vishwaroop thought, perhaps his youngr brother was an incarnation of Lord or he was Himself God.

He regained senses when little Nemai called elder Vishwaroop - 'Dada, Maa is calling you. Meal is ready. Come now, it is high time for meals'.

At that moment Vishwaroop came outside and sought permission from his teacher to return home back with lovely younger brother. Sri Adwaita Acharya who lost senses for a while got senses and looking to his student Vishwaroop and little Nemai and permitted them to go back to their home.

Vishwaroop laughingly accompanied Nemai and holding his hand said - 'Let's go. You could wear at least a dress brother'.

Childhood of Nemai

One day Sachimaa and Jagannatha Mishra both witnessed the divine footprints of little Nemai. As per Vaishnava Abhidhan there at the right foot were Conch, Ring, Arch, Kamadhenu, Barlie Grain, Vacuum, Circle,

Flag, Triangle, Flower, Curved Moon, Pitchers, Small Plant, Mirror, Tortoise, Fish and at the left there were signs of Umbrella, Danda, Lotus, Ankush, Hill, Club, Box, Chariot, Tri-faced Arrow, Pea-cock, Swastika as Square.

Nemai once ate earth instead of sweet given by his mother. When she asked - "Are you eating clay instead of sweet?"

Child Nemai answered - "Nothing is made of other than earth. All the things are altered forms of the earth."

One day, having worn golden ornaments little Nemai was stolen by two thieves one of them was Meghmali by name. But they, could not reach their destination rather by roaming wholl day taking him on the shoulder of one the unknowingly reached the house of Jagannatha Mishra and Sachimaa who were anxious to find Nemai. The thieves dropped Nemai and he ran to his parents. The thieves were fortunate that they could escape easily as they got the grace of Nemai the little God.

Once, little Nemai smelt that, at the houses of Jagadish Pundit and Hiranya Bhagawata some palatable dishes of non-regular foodstuff for observing Ekadashi were being prepared. Nemai insisted Sachimaa to bring those for him. Sachimaa was ashamed of his insisting anybody. Both the pundits however, knowing from unknown sources themselves brought a few dishes at first for giving Nemai.

One day, a Brahmin traveller named Satyabhanu Upadhaya who live on self-cooked rice was welcomed at the house of little Nemai and was given materials for cooking and thereafter offering to Lord Narayana. Little Nemai took some portion of it. The Brahmin could not use the cooked food.

Then little Nemai was kept for sleeping in a room. He again cooked and little Nemai easily could eat the 'Bhog' before offering. The Brahmin thought himself that God does not want that he cook again and so decided to take fruits. But Vishwarup returned home and consoling him assured that the incidence would not occur again.

Now little Nemai was locked in a room but the Brahmin again saw Nemai at the front of offered 'Bhog' as Lord Narayana and advised him not to disclose it. He happily bowed his head to him and took the Prasad. He knew Nemai as Narayana. Afterwards he did not leave Nabadwip to have chance of seeing Nemai regularly.

On a certain day before the 5th birthday little Nemai or Gouranga was playing on the yard of their home in Nabadwip. He was wearing some valuable ornaments on his whole body. Somehow he came out on the main road adjacent to their house and no one could notice it. At that time like other passers-by two thieves were also passing. One of them was ill famed Meghamali. He noticed the precious ornaments on the body of Nemai. Nemai for his fair complexion looked like also a golden boy. The thief became greedy and planned to steal those jwelleries so, picked him up and took him on the shoulder as others carry their children.

His partner asked - "What are you doing ?"

The main thief replied- Do'nt worry, we shall steal the ornaments only and then we leave the child nearer this house. We can earn much money by selling all these golden jwelleries and divide the money in between us, now make haste to find a place where we can hidingly do it.

Both of the thieves taking the child on one shoulder by hanging his feet from two sides and amusing him like other citizens do while carrying children move normally they walked the whole of the town.

On the other hand, at the house of Nemai his father Jagannath Mishra, mother Sachidevi and elder brother Vishwaroop and other neighbours were trying to find their lovable little Nemai. They enquired the houses and every possible place but Nemai was not found.

The thieves, however, could not stop for a while as they did not get any place for taking off the ornaments. It was true that they fed the child with suitable food from shops during the whole day but they could not have any food. They wandered the whole Nabadwip town and were tired with empty stomach. It was almost evening. Suddenly, they found the place from where they picked the child up and fled. They found many people were anxiously waiting for the child. They looked up and saw the divine child Nemai was smiling, as if he indicated to flee. They dropped the child and could disappear. They were saved as Lord smilingly forgave them.

On the other hand all people were pleased to find their lovely Nemai. None could find anyone there.

Little Sri Gouranga or Nemai used to play with a bunch of children like Sri Gadadhara, Sri Mukunda, Sri Murari and others. He used to utter the dialects of Sylhet to those who were from Sylhet origin like him. He used to pronounce their dialects jokingly.

Nemai used to take bath and swim regularly with Gadadhara, Mukunda, Murari and other friends in the water of the Ganga. There usually the girls were worshipping Lord Shiva Mahadeva but Nemai would snatch their garlands to wear. Sri Nemai sometime used to decorate himself with the sandalwood paste and garlands from the girls despite their screaming in objections. Sri Gouranga or Nemai knew well that whoever the gods and the goddesses were being worshipped by the girls all the materials are to go to the Supreme, God of the Universe. Probably one of the girls was Laxmipriyadevi.

He also used to get pleasure by joking and exchanging the clothes from gents' bathing places to another place of female. Sri Gouranga apparently used to disturb others in the 'Ghats' or on the roads.

His friends including Gadadhara (later as Gadadhar Pundit) remained with him but tried to restrain Nemai from all of the jockings.

However, Nemai was scolded and sometime threatened by stick by Jagannatha Mishra.

Both the parents Jagannath Mishra and Sachidevi one day were discussing on the marriage of their elder son Vishwaroop as he was becoming adult. Somehow Vishwaroop learnt it. By reading lot of Scriptures and knowing the life of Shankaracharya Vishwaroop already determined not to bind himself in family life 'Maya' and to become an ascetic. He was sure that there would remain his younger brother Nemai in order to look after their parents. So, without informing anyone one day he left the house for ever and started to wander in the Country as an ascetic in the name Shankaranya.

The whole family including Nemai could hardly tolerate this separation from Vishwaroop. The mother Sachidevi had the pain for separation throughout the life. The father Jagannath Mishra expressed that for the teachings from very learned Adwaita Acharya his elder son became a 'Sannyasi' and he dropped the learning programme for their only remaining son Nemai.

Little Nemai was also an attentive student from very beginning but he was forbidden to go to any learning centre or to take any further lesson. He had nothing to do but to play. Nemai did not like the readingless position of a pupil like him. After a few days, he sat on a heap of rubbish, the spot for dustbin.

His parents and many elderly people from neighbours' houses gathered there and directed to leave the dirty space and to have a bath and wash all the limbs with sufficient water. Yet, little Nemai did not respond.

At last, father Jagannath Mishra came with a cane and ordered. "Come down and wash yourself. Don't you know it is not a place to sit ?"

Little Nemai then laughingly replied - "Dad, You have stopped my learning, studying all and then how I would know what is right or what is wrong?"

Jagannath Mishra and Sachidevi afterwards agreed to allow Nemai to resume in studying. With joy Nemai came down and it is known to all that Nemai, our Gouranga became an unparalleled scholar.

Hindolika Riding with Gadadhar

Renowned researcher Dr. Kananbihari Goswami has mentioned in his writing on Hindolika Vihar from the Manuscript Sri Gourlilamrita or Gouranga Vilas (unpublished) written by Bangshibadan Chattopadhyay (1494 - 1548 AD) at the Periodical of Sahitya Parishat 108 Yrs, 1-4 issue. This book was perhaps written before the completion of writing of *Sri Chaitanya Bhagawata* by Sri Vrindabandas (1508 - 1590 AD). It may be presumed that the writer wrote the Manuscript before 1548 AD before his death.

In this Manuscript Sri Gourlilamrita it was found:-

Vijaya Gouragadadhara Hindolika Manohar
Kandarpa Rathera Shova Jini,
Tahe Kori Aarohan Aarambhila Premran
Aashe Pashe Vktera Saajani. (p. 96 Ka)

So, we find that Sri Gouranga and Sri Gadadhara Pundit were much closed friends from the very beginning. Sri Gouranga travelled the houses of people of different occupations. Sri Gouranga travelled at the houses of ordinary people of different professions and was welcomed by them with warm reception.

One day our beloved Gouranga or Nemai reached the house of a family of milk man. All the people of the house stood and with folded hands in order to welcome Gouranga. Fair complexioned with white sacred thread hanging from his left shoulder. He was wearing a white 'Dhoti' and a small wrapper on his body. To see the divine look Gouranga all the members of the family were highly pleased.

Some of them considered him as Lord Sri Krishna and remembered the known episode that Krishna was once brought up in the family of Nanda, the local king of milkmen in Vrindaban. Nanda had many cows.

Little Krishna was fond of grazing and feeding the calves and the cows. He had also other friends who were from the houses at Braja or Vrindaban.

So the people there took him as their own man and brought some sweets made of milk for Gouranga and his companions.

He received plenty of love and affection from the people of milkmen families. Gouranga knew that these people would be helpful in future in establishing to teach that differentiation among mankind was wrong customs.

Sri Gouranga visited the houses of the people who were dealing in spices and perfumes. The whole community of them were much glad to see him at their locality.One of the perfume substance seller received him cordially and offered him high quality perfumes and in turn Gouranga tried to offer price for the substance but the seller mildly answered - "Don't worry, first you use it. I will take the price later on."

Gouranga was so beloved by everyone since he met.

Once Gouranga had been at the houses of florists. The people there were very happy to find him at their houses. Many of them bowed their heads to offer due respect. They found golden white complexioned with curled long black hair Gouranga as divine personality. Some started to decorate him and his associates with garlands of fragrant flowers. He wanted to refuse but couldn't. The whole atmosphere was full of fragrances.

Sri Gouranga was surprised as all the flowers were made for him. Sri Gouranga received immense love from them.

On foot Gouranga reached the houses where the betel leaf sellers resided. The people there, were highly glad to have the heart of Nabadwip Sri Gouranga. Some of them prepared betel leafs with betel-nut, camphor and other scented materials for chewing Gouranga despite his resistance. All considered themselves fortunate as Sri Gouranga himself chose their houses what they never dreamt of they sang for sometime.

Thus, Sri Gouranga was acceptable by all irrespective of caste or creed.

He had been at the houses of conch sellers. They were also pleased to find Gouranga at there place. One of them gifted a big conch-shell what befitted to divine like look Sri Gouranga only. The conch sellers took him as Lord Narayana has come to them. This happening helped them to consider themselves fortunate. The whole area perhaps was brightened with divine light they thought. Sri Gounmga was so beloved by ordinary people like conch sellers.

Sri Gouranga went to the house of Sarbajna who alone lived at a corner of Nabadwip town. He was pious with enough respect for Lord Sri Krishna. Seeing Gouranga he stood up and greeted him by saying - "Oh, Gouranga please come in and be seated here."

Originally his fore-fathers came from Karnataka State. Out of them in later period were Sanatan, Roop and Jib Goswamis who established Vaishnavism in the light of Sri Gouranga i.e. Sri Chaitanya.

Sarbajna was looking forward to Sri Gouranga. He stayed looking for an unlimited time. All the atmosphere was forgotten by him. He felt that Lord of the Universe in different shapes was sitting at his front. Sarbajna could not speak for hours and cried.

Gouranga just smiled and returned home.

Sridhar was a simple seller of banana leaves and cone at a corner of local market. Gouranga usually bought some cone, green banana and also leaves on which he liked to have meals.

Gouranga was fond of bargaining with him. Sometime he used to snatch his banana leaves from Sridhar.

One day Gouranga visited the house of Sridhar. Sridhar finding Gouranga became pleased and also started to fear.

Gouranga seeing his position told - Do not be afraid of. I shall not snatch your banana leaves or green banana from you today.

Sridhar bowing his head and with folded hands said - "You are a respected and famous teacher in Nabadwip town but I am an ordinary seller of banana cone and others. Please forgive me for any fault unknowingly done by me."

Sri Gouranga replied to him - "No, nothing intentional or unintentionally you have done anything wrong to me." He took a pause and thereafter rejoined - "I have come to see how much wealth you've hidden here."

Sridhar answered - "Sir, I am a poor man."

"Poor man! Ha ha! I have found you are rich enough what a Vaishnava cannot have it." Sri Gouranga replied by saying - "Your devotion to Lord is so immense that surprised me very much. So, you are not a poor man. You have plenty of devotion and a rich person having more enough wealth."

Reality for Family Life

After the demise of his father Sri Jagannatha Mishra (Purandar Pundit) Nemai realised the hard reality of maintaining family day-to-day expenses. So, before completing own education Nemai decided to accept the profession of teaching to students in newly opened Tole (education centure) at the Chandi Mandap of Sanjoy Mukunda. Generally, it remains vacant the whole year except at the time of worshipping Sri Sri Chandi or Sri Sri Durga or others. Nemai was permitted to open a Tole for the rest period.

His method of teaching to students were something in different. He used to teach the students at the 'Ghats' of the Ganga, sometime under any tree, or on any portico of anybody's house or on roads while moving in Nabadwip. Students from distant places started to gather to have brilliant coachings from talented, efficient and learned Nemai Pundit. He achieved countrywide fame in teaching within a short period.

Simultaneously, Nemai Pundit also continued his learning from various scriptures old and new.

He learnt different subjects:-

Previously - Grammar, Literature and Rhetorics from Sri Gangadas Pundit; Philosophy from Sri Sudarshan Pundit; Smriti (Law), Mimangsha (Philosophical treatise) and Astrology from Sri Vishnu Mishra and the Vedas from Sri Adwaita Acharya.

Thus, within the earnings of Sri Nemai it became easy to meet up the expenditure of the family, occasional guests (Atithi - who does not see tithi or date to attend at anybody's house) and students of distant places. There was no longer hardship in the family.

Laxmipriya Devi

Laxmipriya Devi was the first wife of Sri Gouranqa Mahaprabhu the daughter of Sri Ballavacharya Mishra of Nabadwip. Sri Lakshmipriya Devi was born in 1492 AD (1414 Shaka, 899 BS) in Nabadwip. Some also liked to state that Sri Laxmipriya Devi was herself the Mahalakshmi of 'Boikuntha'.

Laxmipriya Devi's beauty was incomparable. Her eyes were without blinking and clear. She used to worship Shiva Mahadeva at the 'Ghat' with folded hands and prayed for a preferable bridegroom. It may also be noted that she having shut up her eyes prayed for a bridegroom like Nemai Pundit.

And after the praying having opened the eys she found young Nemai Pundit in front of her.

Banamali Acharya, an aged person with the title of 'Kaviraj' could feel the emotions of Nemai or Gouranga and also the girl Laxmipriya Devi at the 'Ghat' of the Ganga. He became a matchmaker and adviced Sachi Maa for the marriage of Sri Gouranga and Laxmipriya Devi.

The father of Laxmipriya Devi, Sri Ballavacharya Mishra, was highly pleased to the proposal as the life of Nabadwip Nemai Pundit would be his son-in-law and considered this was his fortune.

On an auspicious evening Sri Gouranga as a bridegroom with his friends and students started for journey by a palanquin and other available carts to the house of Sri Ballavacharya.

Among the companions of the bridegroom there were present Sri Adwaita Prabhu, Sri Chandrasekhar Acharya, Sri Gadadhar Pundit, Sri Sri Baas Pundit, Sri Banamali Acharya and other respectable dignitaries of Nabadwip also.

All the roads were decorated with banana trees and leaves and also with illuminatives. On the both sides of the roads thousands of spectators were eagerly waiting for the procession of Sri Nemai. Lot of flowers and garlands were sprayed on Sri Nemai.

The marriage of Laxmipriya Devi and Sri Gouranga (Nemai) was held in 1502 AD (1424 Shaka, 909 BS). On the next day, Sri Gouranga with Sri Laxmipriya Devi returned to the house of Sachimaa. There, on the both sides of the paths thousands of people assembled to see Gour-Laxmipriya combined and many of them considered themselves as fortunate to find the combined Gour-Laxmipriya like Hara-Gouri. Some commented Indra-Sachi, some saw Laxmi-Narayana and some felt Sita-Ram and so on.

Sachimaa received her daughter-in-law cordially with all the rituals with the help of women like Sri Sita Devi wife of Sri Adwaita Prabhu, Sri Malini Devi wife of Sri Sribaas Pundit, sister Sri Sarbajaya Devi wife of Sri Chandrasekhar Acharya, Sri Ratnabati Devi mother of Sri Gadadhara and wife of Sri Madhab Mishra and also the aged mother of Sri Murari Gupta and other dignified women. All of them were cordially received and they enjoyed much.

Sachimaa was satisfied by thinking that her grief for her late husband Sri Purandar (Jagannath) Mishra has now eased. Her house has become again delightful.

Sri Banamali Acharya and Nemai's lifelong friend Sri Gadadhar Pundit were satisfied to see the combined 'Yugal' Sri Nemai and Sri Laxmipriya Devi and accordingly they congratulated them.

Sri Gouranga also arranged a feast for the Vaishnavas and the poor people in Nabadwip irrespectively deserved or not deserved. And all were fed with their satisfaction.

Sri Laxmipriya Devi on request of Sri Gouranga took up the responsibility of cooking also. Sachimaa remained her side only to co-operate and giving guidance her all along. Laxmipriya Devi used to place the Tulsi leaves with spikes on the 'Bhog'.

It is known that sometime more than one dozen Sannyasis or beggers used to meet Sri Gouranga and he used to invite all of them to have lunch at his house. They, mother and wife would not be surprised to learn the sudden invitation made by Sri Gouranga rather they tried their best to arrange the food and from unknown source the materials in plenty would reach the house. Nemai was then considered as 'Professor-in-Chief or Adhyapak Shiromani' in Nabadwip.

However, while in East Bengal after more than six months the human heart of Sri Gouranga i.e. Nemai Pandit ached for not seeing mother and his wife Srimati Laxmipriyadevi. He felt that there might be any wrong with them. All on a sudden he decided to return Nabadwip. And on return to Nabadwip Sri Nemai knew the news that unfortunately his wife Srimati Laxmipriya devi succumbed at her age about 15 years only in 1506 AD due to snakebite. Mother Sachimaa and others were shocked. He understood the reason of mighty attraction or silent call of mother and possibly of Srimati Laxmipriyadevi at the time of her expiry. He consoled himself and also Sachimaa that everybody should tolerate death on which no human has to do anything.

The separation from Sri Nemai for a long time became so shocking to Sri Laxmipriya Devi that it took the shape of a snake and it has bitten her in 1506 AD (913 BS, 1428 Shaka) and despite the best efforts by available physicians, Ojha's etc. after sometime in Falguna (Madhu Mass) she breathed her last.

Vidyavilas by Sri Gouranga

Naturally many of the educated people of Nabadwip had the fear if Nemai asks a critical question in the presence of other persons in eluding students and so preferred to avoid him. Yet, he used to select only the people who engage themselves in worshipping Lord Sri Krishna only. He had the plan in mind to equip the Krishna loving people later may be given the charges of preaching the glory of Lord Sri Krishna.

A valuable stage was Vidyavilas by Sri Gouranga. He was then known by the scholars of Nabadwip as Nemai Pundit. Nemai Pundit had the habit to judge and to ask question from the scriptures to the scholars and the students whenever he met any of them at the Ghats of the Ganga or at roadsides. Normally the learned scholars were afraid of him that always the might not be ready to reply to uncommon questions all on a sudden. Many of them would avoid the location where Nemai Pundit would be present. They generally used the other roads so that any of them might not face such awkward position of replying to any critical question. Nemai did not see whether the questioned person was aged one.

"Keha Bole Heno Rup Heno Vidya Zar.
Na Bhajile Krishna Kichhu Nahe Upakar."

(Ch. Bh. Adi. Ghap.10)

However, some senior to Sri Gouranga, Sri Sribaas Pundit, a lover and worshipper of Lord Sri Krishna had no fear for Nemai Pundit. He just laughingly and tactfully could tackle any situation. It was also true that, Nemai Pundit had the intention of asking questions from old scriptures only to the people who had love for Lord Sri Krishna or regular worshippers of Lord Sri Krishna. Sri Sribaas Pundit was such a man in Nabadwip.

People like Murari Gupta, Sri Mukunda even Sri Gadadhar Pundit and many of inhabitants in Nabadwip who could not reply readily were advised by him to learn from the authentic sources and to meet him again in the next day.

It is known to all that sense of humour and also joking perfectly are the symbols of learned personality. One day having defeated Sri Murari Gupta, Sri Gouranga said to him - Murari, you are a hereditary physician. You possess enough knowledge in remedies of different ailments. You should take up the profession of your family characteristics and treat the diseased. Then why you are spending time in studying Grammar?"

Murari tried to interrupt but Sri Gouranga again continued his speech - Listen to me. Anybody's cough and cold or indigestion or lever problems cannot be cured by your Grammar."

Sri Murari promptly answered - Alright Nemai. But you are coming from a Brahmin family. You need not study much. You just having a sacred thread on your shoulder and some known Shlokas in lips can take up the profession of Pujas and continue the job as a priest at the houses of the inhabitants of Nabadwip town and that would be sufficient for maintaining your family. Is not it? That also would suit to you."

Laughed Sri Nemai and answered - "Good spelt. Now tell me what chapter in Grammar you have learnt to day in the class?"

Sri Murari without spending any word explained everything he had learnt in the class. Sri Nemai was satisfied with the answers but did not express it first. Rather he made a new clarification from another angle what was not known to Sri Murari. He was surprised to note the talents Nemai had. He also did not express and remained silent. Sri Nemai then took him in his arms for embracing with love for his sincerity in learning.

Sri Murari Gupta in Nabadwip Lila of Sri Gouranga used to treat him in his any ailment. He being a devotee of Sri Ramchandra became one of the beloved associates of Sri Gouranga Mahaprabhu. He was also a renowned poet and wrote *Sri Chaitanya Mongal* (popularly known as Murari Gupta's Kadcha) at first.

In this Vidyavilas stage in Nabadwip nearer friend Sri Mukunda an expert composer and singer the songs on Lord Sri Krishna and a student of Rhetoric in the 'Tole' had an attraction to Nemai Pundit and he was sure that once their friend Nemai would be exposed as the incarnation on this earth.

One fine morning Nemai Pundit caught Mukunda on way to 'Tole' and said - "You know that I am involved in teaching students in Grammar, so I should not ask any question on Grammar. You are an expert in singing and in Rehtoric. Now should I ask any question from this beautiful subject?"

Alankar Bichar Koribo Toma Sane.
Prabhu Kahe Boojha Tomar Zeba Loy Mone.
(Ch. Bh. Adi. Chap.1 0)

Sri Mukunda got some relief and started to debate with Sri Nemai Pundit. He was surprised to note that Nemai Pundit had sufficient access in the subject. Mukunda understood that Nemai Pundit had unbelievable wisdom in Rhetoric and many other subjects.

On another morning while Sri Gadadhara Pundit was busy with plucking flowers and Tulsi leaves in a garden Nemai Pundit saw him and coming nearer caught his hands and asked - "Nowadays you are trying to avoid me? Why? You need not be afraid of me, we are friends and related from age after age. Now are you prepared to reply to my questions?"

Laughingly Sri Gadadhara Pundit replied to him - "I know you are trying to train up all of your companions for future. Alright I shall be careful in learning more and more. Now let me go, my father is waiting for Tulsi leaves and flowers to worship Lord Sri Krishna."

Nemai Pundit having heard the name of Lord remained silent for some time and, thereafter, advised him to come on the next day and learn more for the future.

Prabhu Bole Gadadhara Aaji Zaha Ghar.
Kali Bujhibang Tumi Aasiha Sattwara.
Namaskari Gadadhara Chalilen Gharey.
Thakur Vramen Nagare Nagare.

(Ch. Bh. Adi. Chap.10)

Nabadwip was once being considered the Oxford in India.

Nabadwip Hena Gram Tribhubane Nai.

(Ref. Vrindabandas, 'Ch, Bh, Adi, Chap 2)

Sri Gadadhara Pundit

It is true that the name of Sri Gadadhara Pundit is found in the mantra of Panchatattwa comprising of Sri Adwaita Acharya, Sri Nityananda, Sri Gouranga Mahaprabhu, Sri Gadadhara Pundit and Sri SriBaas Pundit but his name and his other activities are not sufficiently publicized.

Sri Krishnadas Kaviraj in "Sri Sri Chaitanyacharitamrita" narrated Panchatattwa as -

Panchatattwatmakang Krishnang Bhakta Swarupakanm.
Bhakatabatarang Bhaktakhyang Namami Bhktashaktikam.

Again Sri Krishnadas Kaviraj bowed his head as -

Sri Chaitanya Nityanada Adwaita Tinjan.
SriBaas Gadadhara Adi jata Bhaktajan.
- Sabar Charanpadme Kori Namaskar.

(Ch. Ch. Adi. Chap.1&7)

Sri Gouranga was born in the 1407 Shaka on the evening of full moon of the month of Falguna in 892 (Bengali Year) (February-March in 1486 AD) in Nabadwip. Sri Gadadhara Pundit was born in 1408 Shaka on the day of the new moon Boisakh 893 (Bengali Year) (April-May in 1486 AD) in Nabadwip. So, Sri Gadadhara Pundit was one and half months' junior to Sri Gouranga.

"...Madhabera Aar Ek Putra Nadiya Majharey.
Boishakhera Kuhudine Janmalaabh Kore.
Rakhila Tahar Naam Srila Gadadhara.
Srikrishnachaitanya Devera Parshad Prabara.
(Prem Vilas by Nityanandadas, Vilas 24)

Being mad for Lord Nemai like a child tried to penetrate own chest with his nails to find Lord Sri Krishna there. Sri Gadadhara Pundit consoled by saying that - God is in feeling.

Sachimaa observed this that a mere boy only one and a half months junior Sri Gadadhara Pundit could make calm her son Nemai Pundit.

She was so satisfied to Sri Gadadhara Pundit for whom she had enough affection like a son that she said - "Please be with Nemai all the time. Never leave him behind alone."

Boro Tusta Hoila Aai Gadadhara Prati,
E mato Subuddhi Sishu Nahi Dekhi Kati.

She requested Sri Gadadhara Pundit-

Aai Bole Baap Tumi Sarbada Thakiba,
Chhadiya Uhaar Sanga Kothao Na Zaiba.
(Ch. Bh. Madhya Chap. 2)

This Sri Gadadhara Pundit never became separated from his Sri Gouranga. Even at the time of last day at the Gundicha Temple in Puri Sri Gadadhara Pundit accompanied Sri Gouranga and both of them were disappeared. Thus, Sri Gadadhara Pundit kept the words of Sachimaa till his last breath.

Srimati Radharani had only ambition to provide everything including of her own for the happiness of Nandasuta Lord Sri Krishna. Sri Gadadhara Pundit had the likewise ambition to give pleasure to Lord Sri Gouranga i.e. Sri Chaitanyadeva. He was a friend indeed.

Sri Gadadhara Pundit was termed as Srimati Radharani in the Bhaktamal also:-

Sri Gadadhara Pundit Bhaktashakti je Anupa.
Srimad Vishwambharadwoit Sriman Nityananda,
Tin Pravu Sarbashestha Sarba Sukhananda.
Tar Madhye Mahapravu Sri Krishnachaitanya,
Dui Pravura Premaspada Jenha Agraganya.

Again,

Premera Swarupa Radha Vrindabneswari,
Tein Srimadgadadhara Pundit Roopdhari.
Vrindaban Lakxmi Shyamsundar Ballava,
Gouraprem Lakxmi Gora-Anga Kanti prava.
Radhakrishna Dui Tanu Miliya Gouranga,
Gadadhara Sri Radha Dwidharupe Rasaranga.
Sri Radhar Pransama Lalita Sundari,
Nija Naam Tulya Naam Anuradha Kari.
Tenha Sri Radhar Roop Gadadhar Dehe,
Chaitanya Sri Radha Jatha Tatha Mili Rahe.
Sri Chaitanyachndrodaya Natkera Matey,
Ebang Swarup Goswamir Barnanatey.
Sri Radha Sri Gadadhara Nahika Sandeha,
Rukminidevir Saha Mili Kahe Keha...

(Sri Sri Bhaktamal by Krishnadas Babaji ed. by Upendranath Mukhopadhyay published by the Basumati, 5th Edition, p. 21 & p. 29)

Mahapravu Sri Gouranga in the Drama Rukmini Sambad danced as Radharani where Sri Gadahara Pundit danced as Lalita Sakhi. In him Rukmini Devi of Dwaraka and the life's best Lalita were influenced Sri Radhashakti Sri Gadahara Pundit.

All the leading information derived about Sri Chaitanyadev and Sri Gadadhara Pundit were based on the Philosophy of Vaishnava Culture, Srimadvagawata, Srimadbhagwatgita, Kadcha of Swarup Goswami, Kadcha of Murari Gupta (in Sanskrit), the direct experiences of Raghunathdas Goswami, Bidagdha Madhab by Sri Roop Goswami, Bilwamongal's Srikrishna Karnamrita, Bhaktamal by Krishnadas Babaji, Tikka of Sridharswami and other related scriptures that were referred by the authors like Krishnadas Kaviraj, Vrindabandas, Lochandas, Jayananda and others.

Sri Keshav Kashmiri Pundit

Once, a country-wide renowned scholar Kashmiri Keshav Pundit on his journey for defeating the scholars and students and gaining fame halted with his followers, bag and baggage, elephants and horses at Nabadwip, the town of higher education in different branches of Sanskrit, in order to win over all the Pundits. He was a 'Digbijoyee' that meant having won on all the Pundits at different sides of the country.

Sri Keshav Kashmiri Pundit was a learned personality having capacity of composing poems at anytime. He was blessed by Saraswati the goddess of learning. The list of all the scholars were collected by his men at Nabadwip and Nemai Pundit's name topped of the list. Sri Keshav was also surprised to note that Sri Nemai was a teen-aged professor at a famous 'Tole' in Sanskrit Grammar. He laughed himself for some time.

In one fine evening Keshav at the time of loitering on the bank of the Ganga and reached at the 'Ghat' where young Nemai Pundit i.e. Sri Gouranga with fair complexion was seated on a pulpit encircled with his students and some of the associates including, obviously, Sri Gadadhara Pundit and some other people of various beliefs waiting at some distance to hear what Nemai was discussing. Sri Keshav could easily recognize Sri Nemai Pundit of Nabadwip by his fellow men and coming nearer expressed self identity. Then and there, Sri Nemai Pundit stood up and bowed his head to such a senior scholar and welcomed him by offering seats at the 'Ghat'.

He just said - "Oh, you are Nemai, teenaged still and you teach Grammar to junior students!"

Sri Nemai Pundit humbly answered - "Yes sir, I am known as Nemai son of Pundit Jagannath Mishra. I have heard your name, you are also a poet of eminence."

Sri Keshav Kashmiri Pundit with some sort of pride in exposure having seated said - "We should fix a date for our debating in scriptures and literature. You are much younger and having knowledge only in Grammar, yet I am to fight with you and hope it would take no much time in defeating you."

Sri Nemai Pundit replied - "Yes sir, I know you are one of the blessed sons of goddess Saraswati. It is not good to fight with you, nor I should have the courage for arguments with you. But it would be a favour for me having a scope of interaction with you. Let it go now. Let the day come." He was humble in praising Sri Keshav Kashmiri Pundit.

Kanha Tumi Sarbashashtrey Kavitwe Pravin.
Kanha Aami Naba Shishya Pduya Navin.

(Ch. Ch. Adi. Chap. 16)

Sri Nemai rejoined - "Sir, I know you are a poet in repute and have the power to compose poems at any time. See, this is a nice evening, the Ganga is flowing speedily and the pleasant breeze is blowing that makes the environment favourable for composing poems. Would you please read a poem elucidating the Ganga?"

Sri Keshav Kashmiri Pundit replied - "Why not? Listen."

Punditji started to recite a self composed poem of one hundred Shlokas praising the river Ganga. The environment became lyrical with the melodious words and voice of Keshavji. For sometime everyone present there were speechless. None could dare to utter a word. Panditji having taken a pause asked - "How it was? Was not a splendid poem?"

Sri Nemai answered - "No doubt the poem was as good as your lyrical recitation. My brothers all here also liked it. They are much enthusiastic like me."

Panditji said - "Oh nice. See I have won many scholars at different centres of the country. So, I have been awarded the title of 'Digbijoyee'. Hope there is no mistake in my poem!"

Sri Nemai again humbly replied - "Do you like to listen to at least one Shloka? Should I repeat?"

The angry Sri Keshav Kashmiri Pundit replied - "Is it possible to pick up one stanza of it, where I have composed and recited one hundred Shlokas?"

It was for the surprise of the Pundit that Nemai started to recite one stanza of the hundred Shlokas -

"Mahattang Gangayah Satatamidamabhati Nitarang,
Ydesha Sri Vishochcharana Kama/otpatti Subhagas.
Dwitiya Sri Laxmiriba Suranarirchchyacharanaa,
Bhabanibhartyuya Sirashi Bibhabyatyadhutgunaa.

(Ch. Ch. Adi. Chap.XVI)

Sri Keshav Kashmiri Pundit was surprised to note that the young boy within teens could easily cite the stanza from his memory but only having heard the hundred Shlokas once only. He started to think how it could be?

The people who were listening to them shouted eagerly - "Sir, Nemai Pundit you please tell him to explain the meaning in local language."

Sri Nemai again said - "Sir, can you make us understood the meaning of the poem in prose forms? Here are many ordinary people who are not yet involved in the culture of higher education in Sanskrit".

Punditji laughed and replied - "It was a very easy lucid poem. There is nothing more to understand in it. Moreover, I was much careful in using words, prosody, metrical compositions etc. It was praising to the Ganga that was born from the feet of Sri Vishnu now flowing all the time, she is glorious like the second Laxmi and was kept on the head of Shiva Mahadeva and having great qualities. Can you find any laps in the poem at least in the stanza you could remember from memory?"

Sri Nemai humbly replied - "About mistakes? There remain some mistakes in one Shloka only. What about others?"

Punditji was angry and said - "Mistakes! It should not be done by an eminent poet and scholar like me, Nonsense."

Punditji again angrily reacted - "Faults! It can't be. I am the great conqueror scholar in the country. I cannot understand from where you are getting courage to challenge me. You are nothing but an ordinary tiny teacher of Grammar for children."

He again boastingly said to Nemai - "Alright, indicate it in your grammatical outlooks. I am here to listen to you."

Some of his students and the associates including obviously Sri Gadadhara Pundit, Mukunda, Murari, Sribaas and some other people of various beliefs were waiting at some distance to hear the historical debate. All were eagerly waiting for the final decision and so a howling was aroused.

Sri Nemai advised them by raising hands to remain calm and peaceful. Turning towards Sri Keshav Kashmiri Pundit he said "Sir, yes there are a few faults in it. Do not mind Sir, there are five items you have mistaken."

"No, it is impossible" said Sri Keshav Kashmiri Pundit - You are speaking much of it.

Sri Nemai laughed and said calmly - "You have started the verse as 'Mahattang Gangayah' whereas it should be started by putting 'Idang'. The indiscretion fault has been used here. The second is 'Dwitiya Sri Laxmiriba' the rhetoric appears to be lesser weight than Laxmi for the use of 'Dwitiya', the second. The third is 'Bhabanibhartyuya' where only Bhabani indicates wife of Lord Shiva or Bhaba itself. But Bhabani's bhartya implies husband of Bhabani. It was meaningless because in it there remains the scope of presuming that Bhabani possibly had another husband, is not it?"

He also indicated - "The fourth is 'Bibhabyatyadhutgunaa' where the word 'bibhabati' completes the sentence and after completion using an adjective creates the error of repetition in the prosody."

Nemai Pundit paused for a while and looked at the face of Punditji. It was almost red in anger or shame. He could not speak as he did not find any suitable word. On the other hand the students and the associates like Sri Gadadhara Pundit, Sri Mukunda, Sri Murari, Sri Sribaas, Sri Chandrasekhar and some other people surrounding Sri Nemai Pundit shouted again - "Sir Nemai, please tell us more, more." But Nemai Pundit requested them to stop and maintain peace and calmness.

He again said to Sri Keshav Kashmiri Pundit - "The fifth is, in the four lines verse you have decorated only three lines with alliterations but one line was left without any decoration. Is it not a fault for a good poem?"

Sri Keshav Kashmiri Pundit could not lift his head for sometime and was seated as made of stone. The surrounding were shouting and dancing for the victory of Nemai Pundit. Easily having controlled them Nemai said to Keshavji - "Come closer Sir. It was not a debate. Just a short discussion it was. I and you both know that if we try we can also find some grammatical mistakes or lapses in the writings of many great writers too. Let it go. Now the night is deepening so please go back to your residence. You may meet me in the next day."

On the next day, early in the morning Sri Keshav Kashmiri Pundit came to the house of Nemai Pundit and tried to bow his head but Nemai hurriedly lifted him by saying - "Sir, you are an aged scholar, a poet of high reputation in the country. You should not touch my feet rather I should touch your feet." But before doing so Keshav caught him in his arms and said - "In my sleep I dreamt that Devi Saraswati is advising me to consider you as Lord Narayana. Devi Saraswati is wife of Lord Narayana. I am her blessed son. I understood now for that reason Mother Saraswati did not support me."

He wept for a long time and asked Nemai Pundit - "You are the owner of all the creations. I failed to recognize you, please do not mind. Now I am returning. Have you any suggestion for future?"

Nemai Pundit was polite to suggest Kahsavji - "Please never boast for knowledge or wisdom. Take the shelter of Lord Sri Krishna only."

Sri Keshav, afterwards, distributed all his belongings to the poor and the needy and set for touring the pilgrimages with Lord's name Harinaam rest of his life.

Nemai in East Bengal (now in Bangladesh)

The news of defeat of Sri Keshav Kashmiri Pundit was spread in the almost possible places of the country. In Nabadwip the local people were so happy that many of them offered various gifts as presentations to Nemai Pundit. He received those and many of the articles distributed to the poor and the needy families. The news was received at East Bengal (now in Bangladesh), mainly at Vikrampore in the district of Dhaka. There many of the students desired to have coaching from Nemai Pundit.

According to history, the village Panchsar in Vikrampore was a centre of higher education like Varanasi, Mithila, Pune, Ujjain, Nabadwip and other famous centres of the country. In Vikrampore, there took births a good number of important and eminent personalities like Atish Dipankar, of ancient Nalanda Mahavihar. Still today the sons of Vikrampore origin are engaged in many prestigious positions in the world.

"Vidyadwajajnanang Basachya Vikrmpuryancha Bhurimaah"

(Dwigwijay Prakash, in Aamar Vikrampore
by Hari Ananda Barhuri published from
Gyan Publishers, Delhi)

Ultimately, probably in 1505/06 AD Sri Nemai Pundit set for East Bengal accompanying his associates including maternal uncle Sri Chandrasekhar Acharya.

Sri Nemai visited Srihatta (Sylhet) where his paternal house existed. He met his grandparents and relatives in paternal side. Sri Nemai also travelled on both the sides of the river Padma that flows from the Ganga after Maldah and Murshidabad districts (West Bengal - India) and the main distributary channel in Bangladesh. Sri Nemai Pundit was highly delighted to find the beauty and vastness of the Padma. He took the river as the Ganga also. He visited Faridpur, Vikrampore Panchasar. Subarna Village, Egarsindur, Betal Pargana, Dhaka Dakshin and also Sylhet in East Bengal (now in Bangladesh). He also established some education centres (Tole) and arranged the teachers for the future. Thousands of students from different corners attended the centres where Sri Nemai and his deputed associates were teaching with their skills and wisdom.

However, Sri Nemai Pundit advised all the students and other people to take the name of Lord Sri Krishna all the time without leaving all the village gossiping.

Naam Sankirtan Koro Upadesha Koila.

(Ch. Ch. Adi. Chap. XVI)

Once Sri Tapan Mishra came to Nemai and discussed on 'Sadhya Sadhan Tattwa.' Afterwards he opined to be with Sri Nemai Pundit. But Sri Nemai advised him to settle in Varanasi and assured he would meet him there on some day.

Further, it was known that afterwards on way to Mathura-Vrindaban travel Sri Chaitanyadeva met him at his residence in Varanasi. Later Sri Tapan Mishra's son Sri Raghunath Bhatta was considered among one of the 'Six Goswamis' like Sri Sanatan, Sri Roop, Sri Jib, Sri Raghunathdas and Sri Gopal Bhatta. There were also present Sri Krishnadas Kaviraj, Sri Subuddhi Roy. Also there were present Sri Lokenath and Sri Bhugarva Goswamis whom Sri Gouranga had sent earlier in Vrindaban. All of them were given the charges of shouldering the responsibilities of reviving the abandoned temples and the deities of Lord Sri Krishna, Sri Gopal and some others. All the Goswamis were also given the duty of promulgating the Vaishnava Scriptures.

However, after more than six months the human heart of Sri Gouranga i.e. Nemai Pandit ached for not seeing mother and his wife Srimati Laxmipriyadevi. He felt that there might be any wrong with them. All of a sudden he decided to return Nabadwip. And on returning to Nabadwip Sri Nemai knew the news that unfortunately his wife Srimati Laxmipriyadevi succumbed at her age about 15 only in 1506 AD due to snakebite. Mother Sachimaa and others were shocked. He understood the reason of mighty attraction or silent call of mother and possibly of Srimati Laxmipriyadevi at the time of her expiry. He consoled himself and also Sachimaa that everybody should tolerate death on which no human has to do anything.

Nemai Pundit again engaged himself in studying and teaching more and more. There remained almost all the time his intimate friend Sri Gadadhara Pundit, Murari, Mukunda and some others. He could not have any peace or any enthusiasm in remaining at home for a long time. Apparently he was restless. His everyday routine in studying, coaching students in his own way of sitting under a tree or anybody's outhouse or Chandi Mandapa or at the stairs of any 'Ghat' of the Ganga and discussing with his friends.

Nemai's Marriage with Vishnupriyadevi

By seeing Nemai's involvement in studying, coaching and discussing throughout the whole days Sachimaa thought it was because of loneliness without wife. It pained Sachimaa and so she expressed her desire to tie her only son Nemai with worldly 'Maya' i.e. to get him married. She informed Nemai her proposal for arrangement of second marriage. But Nemai showed his unwillingness of marriage. Despite his unwillingness Sachimaa started to find a suitable match for Nemai.

One fine morning at the 'Ghat' of the Ganga while bathing she found Vishnupriyadevi, the daughter of Rajpundit Sri Sanatan Mishra of Nabadwip. She had seen this girl several times at the 'Ghat' of the Ganga bathing and maintaining customary of worshipping Lord Shiva and other gods and goddesses. She preferred her and now looked at her from another angle and realised this girl would be a good match for her son. Nemai having understood mother's eagerness and also loneliness at last agreed to her proposal and an admirer and one of the followers Buddhimanta Khan, a local zemindar spontaneously came forward to shoulder the burdens of costs of the marriage ceremony. All the students including the associates like Sri Gadadhara Pundit, Mukunda and Murari and some others were happy to learn it.

After the marriage the people of Nabadwip saw the couple and compared them as Rama-Sita, some as Hara-Gouri and some as Kamala-Hari. However, nothing could bind as the whole world was waiting for their future leader. On the other hand Sri Nemai did not stop the practice of studying, teaching and discussing throughout whole day with the students and the associates.

Nemai with Gadadhara met People of different Occupations

Sri Nemai Pundit wanted to see all the people of different occupations at different corners of the society. So, he with Sri Gadadhara Pundit had been at the houses of weavers, milkmen, essence makers, conch sellers, betel leaf sellers, banana and cone seller like beloved Sridhar, beggar like Suklambar Brahmachari and many others including migrated from Karnataka a lone worshipper of Lord Krishna Sri Sarbajna Pundit. He with his intimate friend was received cordially. Most of them living behind the castes or creed or origin took him as their own man.

Many of the people worshipped him like God. All the members of their families were so happy that they hurriedly assembled around Sri Nemai and Sri Gadadhara and heartily received even with some small gifts as presentation.

Sri Nemai also embraced all as own with love and affection. It was almost a regular programme of Sri Nemai Pundit with Sri Gadadhara Pundit. Both of them were seen at roaming in the town.

II. Harinaam Sankirtan Mahayajna

Ishwarpuri in disguise arrived at Nabadwip

Meanwhile, Sripad Ishwarpuri, a disciple of the eminent Sripad Madhabendrapuri arrived at Nabadwip in disguise. He was in simple dress without any sign of Vaishnavism like 'Tilaka' on his head, arms etc. in order to avert the people who had some envy feeling enmity against Vaishnavas and also the Hindu others.

He was roaming in the town. But Sri Nemai Pundit could easily recognize him as a pure Vaishnava. He took him at his house and his mother arranged the 'Prasad' of Sri Vishnu at their residence. Similarly, Sripad Ishwarpuri visited the house of Sri Adwaita Acharya who was also a disciple of eminent Sripad Madhabendrapuri. But at first, both of them could not recognize each other. Sri Adwaita Acharya was then busy with worshipping of Lord Sri Krishna so he could not stare at the person who had been at his house. After worshipping Lord Sri Krishna he looked at him having a question about the identity of the comer. Obviously he guessed the person might be pure Vaishnava. At that time Sri Gadadhara Pundit and Sri Mukunda notable singer another bosom friend of Sri Gadadhara were accidentally present there. Sri Gadadhara Pundit hinted Sri Mukunda to sing a song on Lord Sri Krishna. Mukunda started to sing elucidating the glory of Lila of Lord Sri Krishna. On listening to the song sung by Mukunda Sripad Ishwarpuri fell on the floor in ecstasy and fainted. Sri Adwaita Acharya then caught hold him and understood Sripad Ishwarpuri was a genuine Vaishnava. Both disciples of Sripad Madhabendrapuri were introduced with each other and became friends.

He took shelter at the house of Sri Gopinath Acharya for some days.

It was the first visit of Sripad Ishwarpuri in Nabadwip but could easily know Sri Nemai Pundit as his own person and also took Sri Gadadhara Pundit as a loveable young boy for his modesty and sweet behaviour.

At that time Sripad Ishwarpuri was writing a book titled as 'Krishna lilamrita'. He used to read it out to Sri Gadadhara Pundit.

"Gadadhara Punditere Aapanar Krita,
Punthi Parhaen Naam Krishnalilamrita."

(Ch, Bh. Adi. Chap.g)

Almost everyday during the period of some recess from studying, teachings Sri Nemai Pundit would visit him at the house of Sri Gopinath Acharya. There Nemai also received the pleasure of listening to the reading of the book. Sripad Ishwarpuri once requested him to please indicate if any mistake is found in the writing. Sri Nemai Pundit laughed and said to him - "It is on the divine Lila of Lord Sri Krishna. No question of any criticism here arises."

Nemai at Gaya and Initiation from Ishwarpuri

Further, almost after two years of marriage with Vishnupriyadevi in 1427 Shaka Sri Nemai visited Gaya after taking permission from Sachimaa. Sri Chandrasekhar and some of his students and followers accompanied him. There he performed the sacred rituals towards the deceased father and fore-parents including other ancestors. He was advised by his 'Panda' to bow down his head on the Sri Pada of Lord Vishnu and Nemai did so but he was so overwhelmed with ecstasy fell down and fainted. At that time accidentally Sripad Ishwarpuri was present there. He also got the same state somehow controlled himself and took up the body on his lap and nursed him in order to revive normal sense of Sri Nemai Pundit.

Afterwards having observed profound devotion to Lord Sri Krishna in him Sri Nemai had the strong eagerness to have initiation from him. He earnestly begged for initiation in Sri Krishna Mantra to Sripad Ishwarpuri. And he did so. From then Sri Nemai i.e. Sri Gouranga became like a mad for Lord Sri Krishna. Sripad Ishwarpuri also felt himself fortunate by giving initiation in Sri Krishna Mantra to Sri Gouranga.

On return to home at Nabadwip Sri Gouranga a changed person as he forgot to ask question from old scriptures to his associates and the people only Krishna loving. The people like Sri Sribaas Pundit, Sri Ramai, Sri Mukunda and others were talking that Nemai has become changed person. He does not bother to ask anything to anybody. He could find Sri Krishna here and there. As if he played 'hide and seek' with Lord Krishna.

However, he expressed to let others to know his experiences and called some of his associates at the hut of Sri Suklambar Brahmachari in an afternoon. Sri Gadadhara Pundit reached the house of Suklambar Brahmachari and hided in an inner room and remained there in order to listen to what experiences Sri Gouranga shares with others. He had to wait much time and from inside saw the associates were coming to the house one after another.

At last, Nemai i.e. Sri Gouranga somehow stepping slowly and tilting the tall fair body reached the house of Suklambar Brahmachari. He was being fainted repeatedly and Sri Murari or Sri Mukunda tried for lifting him from falling on the ground.

He was not capable of talking with others as his eyes were shedding tears incessantly. Once he himself caught a pillar of the balcony and saved from falling. He was then uttering only "Ha Krishna" and "Ha Krishna" and "Where's He?" and "Where's He?" and nothing more.

Sri Gouranga holding the hands of Sri Murari said - Murari, please worship Sri Krishna. Tell me, would you not worship Lord Krishna? He is nice. He is very sweet. Sadashiv, please come, Mukunda please come we should worship Lord along. Oh, I cannot wait for Lord Sri Krishna, Oh Lord... "

Sri Gadadhara Pundit could not tolerate such condition of his most intimate friend Sri Gouranga and so he without efforts of resisting himself suddenly wailed and cried outburst. Accidentally, Sri Gouranga heard that shouting and asked others - "Who from inside is crying so?"

Sri Gouranga earlier had advised all his associates to join at a meeting at Sri Suklambar Brahmachari's house. He did not invite Sri Gadadhara Pundit separately. And so, probably as childlike with excessive sensitivity Sri Gadadhara Pundit was offended and so he with shyness hided himself inside. But any sort of sorrow of Sri Gouranga was unbearable to him. He could not tolerate such pain as Sri Gouranga was getting and so he cried out.

Murari replied to Sri Gouranga - It's your Gadadhara."

From this reply by Murari it is understood that Sri Gadadhara Pundit was like a shadow of Sri Gouranga. He had the habit of being with Sri Nemai Pundit i.e. Sri Gouranga and he knew always how Sri Gouranga is pleased. He used to serve to him as Srimati Radharani would only be happy to see Lord Sri Krishna happy all the time.

Sri Gouranga and Sri Gadadhara Pundit were like Lord Sri Krishna and Srimati Radharani. They were considered as one soul with two bodies what cannot be segregated. So, Sri Gouranga had no idea to inform earlier Sri Gadadhara individually about the meeting.

Sri Gouranga then and there called Sri Gadadhara Pundit to come outside. Sri Gadadhara Pundit was still crying in himself in anxiety of the pain of Sri Gouranga was feeling.

Sri Gadadhara Pundit came out with folded hands from inside the room. Seeing Sri Gouranga lying on the floor he nursed and thereafter lifted him. Sri Gouranga then spoke to him -

Provu Bole Gadadhar Tumi Je Sukriti,
Shishu Hoite Krishnate Karila Drirhmati.

(*Sri Amiya Nemai Charit*
by Mahatma Sisir Kumar Ghosh 1/8)

Sri Gouranga then told Gadadhara - "You are from very childhood engaged with worshipping Lord Sri Krishna. You are a fortunate devotee."

He again started to state - "I've seen and got Lord Sri Krishna in my front but I couldn't catch Him. Oh, Lord... .."

Sri Gouranga was not able to speak any more and was to fall down on the ground and Sri Gadadhara Pundit somehow with the help of Murari-Mukanda-Suklambar Brahmachari caught him.

Shyamang Hiranyaparidhing...

One day, Sri Gouranga was coaching the students in the portico of the house of Sri Ratnagarva Pundit. Generally, he used the Chandi Mandap of Mukunda-Sanjoy, or anywhere under any tree or at any 'Ghat' of the Ganga. This day he had the mood of coaching while walking on roads and after some walking he paused at the portico and continued coaching. With him Sri Gadadhara Pundit and some other associates were also present. He was completely absorbed in teaching the students but he heard a verse nicely recited by Sri Ratnagarva Pundit who was returning home. Nearer to the house he was reciting from Srimad Bhagawata -

Shyamang Hiranyaparidhing Banamalyabahardhatu,
Prabala Natabeshamanubratangshe,
Vinyasta Hastamitayena Yunamabjam,
Karnotpala Kapola Mukhabjalasam.

(Srimad Bhagawata. Sk 10. Chap. 23 Shloka 22)

Sri Gouranga having listened to the verse could not resist his feelings. He was overwhelmed by seeing in mind Lord Sri Krishna appeared in front of him. His complexion was alike the clouds full of water. He was wearing clothes in yellow colours, garlands of flowers of various colours and shape emitting different sweet fragrances around neck, on head there remained pea-cock's beautiful feather. He wore some ornaments made of gold, coral and jewels. He looked like an actor of a drama of the Universe.

He resting left hand on a shoulder of one of the companions and with another hand was circling a lotus of His divine Lila. He had a piece of smile in between the coloured lips. Shinning earrings were hanging from the ears. Some pieces of silk like hair were also hanging on the cheeks and the face. He was looked marvelously.

Sri Gouranga having witnessed Lord Krishna in front him tried to hold but fainted and fell on the floor but could not resist from falling. He was hurt. The students and Sri Gadadhara Pundit after spraying water on his face tried to bring back his senses and lifted him. Sri Gouranga woke up but could not sit erect and requested Ratnagarva Pundit - "Please recite the verse again Pundit Ratnagarva. Please do it."

Sri Ratnagarva Pundit, son of Sri Nilambar Chakraborty and brother of Sachimaa was conversant in Srimad Vagawata. Almost out of 18,000 verses of the Mahapurana and without wasting any moment he started to repeat - "Shyamang Hiranyaparidhing... .."

Sri Gouranga in ecstasy began to witness the divine beauty of Lord Sri Krishna in front of him and again he was becoming unconscious. To see the condition of friend Nemai Sri Gadadhara Pundit with folded hands requested the maternal uncle of Nemai Sri Ratnagarva Pundit - "Please, do not recite the verse again. Please stop recollection and recitation. Our Nemai mentally is unable to bear the situation. He's ill. We are to nurse him now and take him back to Sachimaa safely."

With the help of Gadadhara and the students Sri Gouranga stood up and embraced Ratnagarva Pundit by saying- "It was the finest of verse." He also asked him - Why you have stopped the recitation?"

Sri Gadadhara Pundit himself replied to Sri Gouranga - He stopped as I requested. Because by listening to him you were becoming ill in ecstasy. Our duty is to take you safely to Sachimaa. Now let us go back."

Sri Gouranga's Madness Enhanced

Sri Gouranga's madness enhanced for Lord Krishna like Srimati Radharani in Braja. In this condition of deliriously asking for Lord Krishna Sri Gouranga was almost unable to coach the students so, he failed to attend at the 'Tole' or at the 'Ghat' or at any place for un-precedent self-introduced system of teaching schedule. On the other hand at home Sachimaa felt some trouble to meet up the costs of running the family expenses. At that time the family of Sri Gouranga in addition to normal members' there would almost regularly presence of the guests coming from different places of the country without notice and also the students. This financial burden could be met only by earning but the only left son Sri Nemai had no worry for the family.

However, the neighbouring people who were truly well wishers and some of them were also relatives forwarded their helping hands. Some senior personalities also humbly requested to coach the students for the future. They preferred his novel system of teaching.

In the meantime, like other well wishers Sri Krishnananda Agambagish, a devotee of the mother Sri Kali, who renovated the shape of modern present Kali Murti, goddess of power, came to the house of Sachimaa. He was some senior student of the 'Tole' where both of them studied and humbly advised Sri Nemai Pundit to take care of the family first and thereafter, to worship Lord Sri Krishna.

Sri Gangadas Pundit, his teacher from the very beginning who lived nearer tried to convince Sri Gouranga at least to attend the classes he had started. Thousands of students from distant places were waiting for novel teachings of him.

At Last, Sri Nemai admitted the saying of Sri Gangadas Pundit who suggested and restarted to take classes in his novel system of teachings. Sri Gadadhar Pundit was the prime witness of all these happenings.

However, the same state of mind of Sri Gouranga was continuing. Sri Gouranga used to cry in delirium like Srimati Radharani and His 'Sakhis' who were left behind by Sri Krishna when He with elder brother Sri Balarama was taken by Sri Akrur (not crur-cruel) to Mathura the Capital of King Kansa.

Afterwards, Uddhab an associate of Sri Krishna in Mathura was sent to observe the condition of up-bringer parents Sri Nandaraja and Srimati Jashoda maa. He was also to see how the days were passing by Srimati Radharani and His 'Sakhis' in Vrindaban who were left behind. Sri Uddhab witnessed them in utter grief-stricken condition that was never ending.

Sri Radhar Pralap Zoichhe Uddhab Darshane,
Sei Mata Pralap Kore Ratridiney.

(Ch. Ch. Adi. Chap. XIII)

Such was the condition of Sri Gouranga. He was almost mad and younger Sri Gadadhara Pundit only could control him to bring him back in normalcy.

Sri Gouranga's Planning

Sri Gouranga was in search of a way to bring unity and integration to all the people irrespective of caste and creed, the poor or the rich, the illiterate or the wise. He had no other ways to unite the people of the society. All the people were segregated from each other with their different practices and behaviours. They were in practices of defaming others, teasing the innocent people, charging to any person who did some behave against the extant rules of the society and getting money as penalty, or to outcast from society to those who did or mistakably any wrong in their eyes. Thus, the society was almost broken. Sri Gouranga wanted to wipe out all the irregularities of the society. Otherwise the society was becoming lean day after day. Thousands of people suffered with torture by the so-called Samajpatis.

Many of them, thousands in number, preferred to take shelter in other beliefs. He wanted to fight against such systems from the society. He was in search of a way. He knew that no power could fight without any weapon against them and the Administration. He was in search of a way to fight that could meet up their causes of torture and injustice. At last, he got an idea to unite all the people irrespective of castes and creed that could be like a shield. It was nothing but to unite to welcome all at the Harinaam Sankirtan.

Harinaam Sankirtan

Harinaam Sankirtan was at first introduced by Sri Gouranga. He was successful in gaining the faith by all the people of the country. Chanting of God's name Harinaam Sankirtan was started at the house of Sri Gouranga in presence.of Sachimaa and Vishnupriyadevi. After a few days Harinaam Sankirtan was being done at the house of Sri Chandrasekhar Acharya for a few days. Lastly, Sri Sribaas Pundit welcomed the 'whole team' at his more spacious house in Nabadwip. This was known by the Vaishnavas as Sribaas Angan. Many followers who were waiting for such platform of chanting Harinaam Sankirtan started to gather and participate in Sankirtan.

Sri Sribaas Pundit then arranged a ceremonial washing (Abhishek) of their leader Sri Gouranga of the Harinaam Sankirtan and all began to call their loving Nemai Pundit in the name of Sri Gouranga Mahaprabhu.

There were no questions of any caste or creed. All the people who had the faith in God were accepted in the Harinaam Sankirtan Mahayajna. It did not take much time for its circulation. The news spread all over the country shortly.

There were regular participants like Sri Sribaas Pundit, Sri Gadadhara Pundit, Sri Ramai Pundit, Sri Sriman Pundit, Sri Mukunda Pundit, Sri Murari Pundit, Sri Sadashiba Pundit, Sri Suklambar Brahmachari, Sridhar Pundit, Sri Purushottam and many others from Nabadwip and some were from distant places. One of them was Sri Pundarik Vidyanidhi of Chittagong (now in Bangladesh). Admission into Sribaas Angan for Harinaam Sankirtan was not restricted for those who loved Lord Sri Krishna. For castes, creed, poor, rich, learned, illiterate any differences were not counted in welcoming in the Mahayajna.

Sri Gouranga-Gadadhara at Sri Adwaita Acharya

On the other hand, Sri Adwaita Acharya who had residences at Nabadwip and also at Shantipur was eagerly waiting for a savior of the tortured people of the society. He found that there was no one to come up to wipe out all the irregularities and injustice in the society.

At that time the conditions of the people of the country were much deplorable. There thefts, snatchings, robberies or committing dacoities, lootings, killings, rapes, riots, burnings, forced converting into other religion; considering of the poor and the rich, the learned or the illiterate, caste low and high, the thousands of discriminatory treatments among the people jeopardizing the society and the country.

Sri Adwaita Acharya had belief that God Himself would incarnate in this world as He assured in the Sri Madvagawat Gita :-

Yada Yadahi Dharmyasya Glanirbhabati Bharata,
Abhyuthanamadharmasya Tadatmanang Srijyamyaham.
Paritranaya Sadhunang Vinashaya Cha Duskritam,
Dharma Sansthapanarthaya Sambhabami Yuge Yuge.

(Sri Madvagawat Gita 4/7,8)

Sri Adwaita Acharya was expecting that out of themselves one person or a group of persons would come up to relieve the pains and sorrows of the people including ordinary people. Somehow he received the news that Sri Gouranga, then known as Sri Gouranga Mahapravu has started the Yajna for Harinaam Sankirtan. He remembered that at the time of teaching

Vishwarup in the 'Tole' run by him at Nabadwip little Nemai younger brother of Vishwarup occasionally would come to his centre to call back his elder brother.

Seeing all associates in at Nabadwip were stirred with Harinaam Sankirtan, Sri Gouranga and Sri Gadadhara decided to meet seniormost Sri Adwaita Acharya at Shantipur where he was worshipping Lord Krishna with 'Tulsi' leaves and the water of the Ganga. He, after having been informed of Harinaam Sankirtan has already started, was also expecting that soon he would be welcomed.

Sri Gouranga and Sri Gadadhara Pundit both came to Shantipur to meet seniormost Sri Adwaita Acharya. Sri Vrindabandas has described as:-

Ekdin Prabhu Gadadhara Kori Sange,
Adwaita Dekhite Prabhu Range,
Adwaita Sabhay Gelen Duijan,
Dekhila Adwaita Kare Tulsi Sechan.

(Ch. Bh. Madhya. Chap. 2)

To see Sri Gouranga and Sri Gadadhara Pundit both at his residence Sri Adwaita Acharya were so pleased that he could not speak for sometime. Yes, he was waiting for this day. Hurriedly he went to inside the room and brought all the materials for worshipping Sri Gouranga Mahaprabhu. He with folded hands worshipped him with formal rules. He bowed his head several times at the feet of Sri Gouranga as considered him as God. Sri Adwaita also welcomed Sri Gouranga Mahaprabhu as the leader for the movement of Harinaam Sankirtan and Vaishnavas.

(Recently a combination of statues comprising of Sri Adwaita Acharya worshipping Sri Gouranga Mahaprabhu and another Vaishnava (Govinda Duta) playing on Mridanga have been installed by the Panihati Municipality at the traffic island at Sodepur connecting Panihati and B.T. Road.)

He realised that the 52 years' younger Nemai now known as Sri Gouranga Mahaprabhu understood the pains and sorrows of the people tortured at the desires of the people of upper class and society. Sri Adwaita Acharya for the last several years has noticed all these and so, he himself lonely engaged for worshipping Lord Krishna with 'Tulsi' and the water of the Ganga. He also wanted to do welfare work in every respect for irrespective of castes and creed, the poor and the rich, the learned and the illiterate. Because he had the belief that Sri Gouranga had to love all and thus love to Sri Krishna could be successful.

After the usual worshipping Sri Gouranga greeted Sri Adwaita Acharya by saying humbly - "I am fortunate that you have the kindness for me."

Sri Adwaita Acharya replied humbly - "Our Gour, I shall be with you all the time. You are God. You are the Rescuer. You would save the society, the religion of love and the country. I am at seventy two yet I can walk miles after miles. I am not only supporter of Harinaam Sankirtan Movement I am also an active companion. Do not worry. I am with you, perhaps Sri Krishna desires it."

Sri Gouranga Mahaprabhu with Sri Gadadhara Pundit returned Nabadwip as if they were allowed to continue Harinaam Sankirtan Movement with much more enthusiasm.

Harinaam Sankirtan Movement Geared up

Harinaam Sankirtan Movement led by Sri Gouranga Mahaprabhu at Sri Sribaas Angan was geared up. Thousands of people of Nabadwip and its adjacent areas started to assemble and to participate in Harinaam Sankirtan. All of them forgot to note 'who was from Shudra or Chandal or Brahmin families', 'who was pauper or rich', 'who was an illiterate or highly a learned person'.

Sri Gouranga Mahaprabhu then started to roam in the houses of people known or unknown to circulate innocent Sankirtan of Harinaam. All knew to be united and to remain as united in the Sankirtan, Sankirtan of Harinaam.

He also assured all that no one should fear if the men of Administration run by Sultan Hussaein Shah at the court of Murshidabad would attack Nabadwip as the opponent people were trying to threaten the Vaishnavas. He assured them that only harmless Sankirtan of Harinaam would save all in this earth from any obstacles.

Practically, the men and the women, many of taking their children in arms of Nabadwip joined the Harinaam Sankirtan Movement. This was the first in the history that all irrespective of any position they had in earlier society got the opportunity to say 'we are united' by Sri Gouranga Mahaprabhu and his Harinaam Sankirtan Mahayajna.

In the Harinaam Sankirtan Mahayajna Sri Gouranga Mahaprabhu at different stages of the Sankirtan would cry for Lord Krishna, sometime would be fainted in ecstasy for love of Sri Krishna. He also witnessed Lord Sri Krishna. Lord Sri Krishna wearing golden coloured dress with dark black complexion, black hair tied with peacock's colourful feather, ornaments with gems, stones etc. having the eternal flute in one hand, wearing around the neck garlands 'Vaijayanti', 'Koustava', pearls and precious stones, having at the feet around jewels studded anklets came and embraced him. His face was full of smiles.

After regaining sense being patiently nursed by Sri Gadadhara Pundit and other closet participants Sri Gouranga advised all of them:-

Bhaja Krishna Smara Krishna Shuna Krishna Naam,
Krishna Houk Tomara Jiban Dhan Pran.

(Ch. Bh. Madhya. Chap.2)

Sri Gouranga Mahaprabhu having seen lord Krishna coming to him and embraced him but within a moment He was vanished. So, he cried and tears were flowing from the eyes incessantly. He uttered in delirium - Where is He? He received me but now I cannot find Sri Krishna. Gadadhar and the friends, tell me where He is now?"

Again he cried and fell on the ground of Sribaas Angan. All the associates rushed to him and nursed to cure Sri Gouranga Mahaprabhu from fainting.

Many of the associates and all other devotees were anxious about the occasional mental state of Sri Gouranga Mahaprabhu went to Sri Adwaita Acharya and informed him the happenings to Mahaprabhu. His falling on grounds and repeated fainting in ecstasy including crying for Lord Sri Krishna were in the discussion they reported for any solution. Sri Adwaita answered nothing but assured them that he would be present in the Harinaam Sankirtan Mahayajna soon and find, if there is any wrong. Ultimately Sri Adwaita himself became an important participator in the Harinaam Sankirtan Mahayajna.

Sachimaa having observed the restlessness what was increasing in her son Nemai tried her best to cure as the relatives and the neighbours suggested treatment time to time, but failed. Then she went to nearer senior Sri Sribaas Pundit for any way of relief for the ailment.

Sri Sribaas Pundit, in the mean time, was convinced that the Movement introduced by Sri Gouranga Mahaprabhu people of all sections were being united and that unity was the urgent and the most wanted thing for the country. So, he replied to older Sachimaa that for the name of Lord Sri Krishna Sri Nemai has become mad in the eyes of ordinary people. This kind of madness is also like dreams of him and hundreds of devotees. He, thus consoled Sachimaa and assured her not to be worried.

Haridas

Another important inclusion to make the Harinaam Sankirtan Movement towards success was a devotee named Haridas who was welcomed by Sri Gouranga Mahaprabhu. Haridas was born in 1371/72 Shaka (while Sri Gouranga was born in 1407 Shaka) at Burhan village of Nadia district. His parents were Sri Sumati Thakur and Srimati Gouridevi. But unfortunately his father Sumati Thakur had to welcome an immature death. His mother Gouridevi had no closed relatives who would see her and her only son Haridas. Ultimately she, finding no way of living husbandless in the evil effected society spontaneously accepted her death by lying at the side of deceased husband on the funeral pyre. So little Haridas only six years' old became helpless to live in the society where no one wanted to offer him shelter and food.

At last, a kindhearted noble Muslim person of Ambua region Moulana Moloy Kazi took him for looking after the helpless boy. He was brought up in a Muslim family and so he was familiar as Yaban Haridas with others. He had interest in reading scriptures of the Hindus and naturally also of the Islam. He understood that God is one having various names according to various beliefs.

Afterwards, when he grew up he opted to utter Harinaam Mahamantra and took initiation from Sri Adwaita Acharya. He started to take Harinaam three lakh times a day. He was forced to leave uttering Harinaam and to become a holy Muslim. A local Kazi inspired by other people of the community ordered for punishment by lashing with ferules. Yet, at in any adverse circumstances he did not leave Harinaam from his lips.

Khanda Khanda Hoi Deha Jaay Yadi Pran,
Tabu Aami Badane Na Chhari Harinaam.

(Ch. Bh. Adi.Chap.14)

Harinaam Mahamantra was the main source of Sadhana of Sri Haridas Thakur. He; knowing the Harinaam Sankirtan Mahayajna is on progress at Sribaas Angan came to Sri Gouranga Mahaprabhu and Mahaprabhu embraced and accepted him cordially. Sri Gadadhar Pundit, like a shadow follower of Sri Gouranga Mahaprabhu, was also happy to see such a pure lover of Lord Sri Krishna as Haridas has been included in the Harinaam Sankirtan Mahayajna.

Harinaam Sankirtan Mahayajna or Movement got momentum and many people were interested in the new movement without any weapon.

Inclusion of Sri Nityanandaprabhu as Abadhoot

Sri Nityananda Prabhu as abadhoot had travelled more than 20 years since his twelve years' of age in the whole India and lastly reached Vrindaban. Somehow he knew that Nabadwip of Bengal has become flooded with Harinaam Sankirtan Mahayajna or Movement he returned to Nabadwip. He also knew that some people who loved Lord Sri Krishna are with Sri Gouranga Mahaprabhu in the Harinaam Sankirtan in order to enhance the Movement liked to join the team at Sribaas Angan. However, at first he did not speak anybody about his existence in Nabadwip.

Sri Gouranga Mahaprabhu had dreamt in the previous night that a person climbing down from a chariot came to him. He was strong and with bigger bodied. He dressed navy blue coloured clothes. He addressed in dream that he would meet him. However, Sri Gouranga Mahaprabhu sensed that a strong person would come and attend the Harinaam Sankirtan Mahayajna. But he did not get any information and so he sent Sri Haridas and Sri Gadadhar Pundit to find if there was any person waiting for.

Sri Gadadhar Pundit and Sri Haridas tried their best to have information about any stranger has come or not but they returned back without any such information. At last, Sri Gouranga Mahaprabhu with Sribaas, Sri Gadadhara Pundit, Mukunda, Sri Haridas and other participants at Sribaas Angan began to walk direct towards the house of Sri Nanadan Acharya as if he knew where the person could hide himself.

Sri Gouranga Mahaprabhu found, tall strong and stout man having the navy blue coloured dresses an unknown Abadhoot was seated erect at the portico of the house of Sri Nanadan Acharya. There the slope of the thatched shed almost was touching his head.

Sri Gouranga Mahaprabhu and Abadhoot Sri Nityananda Prabhu both looked at each other without any word. They looked for some time and the others including Sri Gadadhara Pundit were also looking at them. All thought that a bold and strong personality like Abadhoot Sri Nityananda Prabhu has come to serve Sri Gouranga -the Harinaam Sankirtan Mahayajna.

After a pause, in order to testify whether this new comer would be able to fight against the evils of the society and to circulate Harinaam among the people Sri Gouranga Mahaprabhu directed Sribaas Pundit to cite any verse from the Bhagawata in order to find the reaction of the new comer. He and all other companions also were waiting to see the result of the testifying of the stranger and the guest at the house of Sri Nandan Acharya. After a short discussion with Sri Gadadhara Pundit, Sribaas Pundit then began to cite from memory a single verse from the Venugeet in the 10th Skandha:-

Borhapeeang Natabarabopuh Karnao Karnikaram,
Bibhadwasha Kanaka Kapishang Boijayanticha Malam,
Randhran Venordhara Sudhaya Purayan Gopavrinderoi
Vrindaranyang Swapadramanang Praabishad Geetakirtih.

(The Madvagawata Mahapuran
by Sri Vyasdev 10/11/5)

As listened to Sribaas's recitation from the Bhagawata Skandha, Chap XXI, Verse V and all they visualised in inner eyes that with the Gopa friends dressed in yellow colour Sri Krishna is entering into the garden of Vrindaban. He is moving in rhythmic stepping. The divine body is itself with the presence of all the rhythms. He appears as the best of all the actors. His head is decorated with peacock's feathers. Two golden earrings are glittering. A Vaijayanti garland is dangling around His neck. He is pouring nectar of divine lips into the divine flute and celestial sound is spreading all over the sky and the Universe. The Gopa friends are singing the songs that are glorifying Lord Sri Krishna. His each and every step was transforming the forest of Vrindaban a holy and beautiful place worth to be worshipped by the gods and goddesses in Heaven and Baikuntha.

Sri Nityananda and all the present could visualise this divine scene and became overwhelmed. Suddenly, the stout, tall and sun-tanned fair complexion bodied Sri Nityananda fainted and fell down on the ground. It was his reaction of the divine scene he visualised. Sri Gouranga Mahaprabhu to note the reaction of the new comer became confident that the person was the right man on whose broad shoulders the responsibility of Harinaam Sankirtan Mahayajna can be set.

Thus, to Sri Nityanandaprabhu was welcomed in the team comprising of Sri Chandrasekhar, Sri Gangadas Pundit, Adwaita Acharya, Sri Gadadhara Pundit, Sribaas Pundit, Sri Ramai Pundit, Sri Mukunda, Sri Murari, Sri Sadashiba, Sri Purushottama, Sri Sridhar, Sri Suklambar Brahmachari, Sri Banamali Acharya and other hundreds associates of Sri Gouranga Mahaprabhu.

Pundarik Vidyanidhi and Sri Gadadhara's Initiation

Another inclusion of Pundarik Vidyanidhi was also an interesting episode. Sri Gouranga Mahaprabhu while absorbed in the Harinaam Sankirtan Mahayajna occasionally used to shout by calling - 'Pundarik',

'Pundarik' and 'Pundarik' my father, the 'Bap' aamar". The associates used to look each other indicating question but all remained answerless. Sometime Sribaas, Sri Gadadhar Pundit and some others who were comfortable in the thousand names of Lord Vishnu tried to guess that this Pundarik might be the name of Lord Vishnu as one of the thousand names He had.

All of a sudden singer mainly on Lord Krishna and a bosom friend of Gadadhara Pundit Sri Mukunda came to him and asked him whether he would accompany him in order to witness a pure Vaishnava.

Gadadhara was much surprised because he has seen Sri Gouranga, he has seen his father Sri Madhab Mishra, Sri Adwaita Acharya, Sribaas even Sripad Ishwarpuri and many more Vaishnavas. He could not reply for some time. He thought to himself who would be such virtuous in practice pure Vaishnava for visiting him Sri Mukunda was informing him?

Sri Mukunda again said to him - "Get ready. Quick and quick; otherwise we would be late to return."

- "Alright" Sri Gadadhara Pundit replied - "I have already seen my father, Sri Adwaita Acharya, Sribaas Pundit and our beloved Sri Nemai. They are real Vaishnavas, as I believe. Yet, I should not miss the opportunity of visiting another virtuous in practice pure Vaishnava. But we should return before Nemai enters in the Sribaas Angan. Is not it?"
- So, I am controlling you to be more responsive. "Quick" Mukunda commented - "No more delay to do. Please hasten your movement."

After walking almost two to three miles (1.6 kms =1 mile) along with Sri Mukunda Dutta, Sri Gadadhara Pundit reached in the afternoon a canopied place where well-dressed a handsome person with rich clothes and costly scarf and having worn on arms valuable ornaments made of gold and jewels was seated by bending lazily on soft fringed pillows. He was surrounded by some visitors and a team of singers and players of 'Mridanga' (one kind of drum), flute, 'Karatal', 'Kanshi' and some other instruments in vogue. The person was chewing betel leaves with rich fragrant spices and was spitting spittle on a spittoon. There in order to give relief from heat from back sides two persons were fanning with peacock's feathers made hand fans all along. Some devotees were spraying cold and fragrant water on him. The state of the ambience was filled with the devotees' queries and talks here and there. In this rich fragrant and luxurious environment that person was seated as a luxurious King.

Sri Gadadhara was brought here by Mukunda to meet a pure Vaishnava but this king-like person at first sight appeared to be a rich Zaminder only. His first look disappointed him. He knew Vaishnavas are generally seen simple in appearance as he had seen Sri Madhab Mishra, Sri Adwaita Acharya, Sribaas even Sripad Ishwarpuri and also Sri Gouranga Mahaprabhu. He knew since his childhood Vaishnavas prefer minimum earthly materials according to their needs to run own families. But this person was not simple like them. He could not be satisfied and was suspicious about the person being a real Vaishnava.

Sri Mukunda having stared to Gadadhara from sitting at the corner meant for the singers and the musicians of different instruments noticed dissatisfaction in the face of Gadadhara Pundit. It was troublesome for him to cross the gatherings and to reach nearer to Gadadhara. He felt that being frustrated with richly gesture Sri Gadadhara would call him with a request to return back or he himself would alone leave the place.

But Mukunda was fully confident that Pundarik Vidyanidhi was a real Vaishnava. He knew him well from his childhood. He realised to do something so that Gadadhara Pundit gets back his confidence in Pundarik Vidyanidhi. He also had the responsibility to make understand Gadadhara Pundit that Pundarik Vidyanidhi was a real Vaishnava and lover of Lord Krishna.

Sri Mukunda remembered Lord Sri Krishna and picked up the first and one of the incidences of His Leelas. It was of only six days' baby after kindly taking birth in this world. Suddenly Mukunda started a song on Rakshas Putana who tried to kill the baby Krishna :-

Tashmin Stanang Durjarabeerymulwanng
Ghorankamadaya Shishorddabha
Garahng Karavyang Bhagawan Prapeedya Tat
Pranoih Samang Roshasamanwitohpibat.

(The Madbhagawata Mahapuran
by Sri Vyasdev 10/6/10)

Putana was a kind of virous of disease for newly born babies. Here in the Sri Madbhagawata Mahapuran Putana was female demon. She was instructed by King Kansa who considered Sri Krishna as his foe and guessing Lord Krishna might have taken birth in Gokul nearer to his capital Mathura to take away the life of new born babies. Lord Krishna there was born just five days earlier. On the sixth day she in disguise of an aristocrat wearing valuable dresses and ornaments lady visited the house of Nanda King of

Gopas at Gokul. He and his wife Yashoda knew that a male baby was born to them. Mother Yashoda could not hesitate to welcome Putana apparently an aristocrat lady who might be from a distant relative. She for an urgent piece of work for a few moments went inside the house and easily trusted on her to leave the baby alone there.

Putana finding the baby alone took him up in her lap and poured her one of the breasts earlier applied with fatal poison in the mouth of baby Krishna. She was sure only by touching her poisoned breast this baby would immediately die as King Kansa desired.

However, the six day's baby was Lord Himself. He knows everything of the past, future and the present. He is the creator and also Himself of the Universe. Having known what is to be happened baby Krishna held her breast with two little palms with anger and ultimately bit with the gums.

Keeng Punah Shrddhaya Bhktya Krishnaya Paramatmane,
Jachchan Priyatamang Keeng Nu Raktastanmataro Zatha.

(Srimad Bhagawata Mahapurana
by Sri Vyasdev 10/6/36)

It was so serious and painful that Putana, the female demon could not tolerate the bite of only six days' baby and died within a moment. With tremendous sound the whole body taking little Krishna on her chest went to high and fell on the ground. Her real appearance was revealed shortly. All coming closer found little Krishna fearlessly was playing and laughing on the chest of Putana but the demon was lying dead.

However, Lord Krishna gave Putana a prestige of a mother. It was His greatness.

Padavyang Bhakta Hridisthabhyang Bandyavyang Lokbanditouih,
Angang Zasyah Samakramya Bhagawapibat Stanam.

(Srimad Bhagawata Mahapurana
by Sri Vyasdeva 10/6/37)

All present including Sri Pundarik Vidyanidhi could easily feel His greatness. The melodious song of Mukunda was on the greatness of Lord that He ultimately gave respect of a mother to Putana also. Sri Pundarik Vidyanidhi also started to sing in the same tune with Mukunda. Sri Vidyanidhi also started to dance in joy and love to Sri Krishna. He recollected from his reading the child Leela of Lord Krishna at His six. He and others at present sang and danced. He was dancing and jumping like a mad and all the materials of luxury, the canopies, the pillows, his dresses, the water spraying bottle, the fans, the betel leaves and fragrant spices were being disarranged or broken by his jumping and dancing. He did not care but fell down on the muddy floor. He was fainted. Seeing Sri Vidyanidhi fainted, Mukunda and all other musicians ran to him. Sri Vidyanidhi who in reaction of the subject sang by Mukunda danced and ultimately fell down and fainted. It was a great surprise to Sri Gadadhara Pundit. Sri Gadadhara also with the eyes filled with tears approached him and repented himself that he earlier did not consider him a real Vaishnava. He thought to himself - "Pundarik Vidyanidhi is a real devotee Vaishnava. Must I seek mercy from him as I have done 'Vaishnava Aparadha' by considering him by seeing his only outer gesture and luxurious appearances."

Sri Gadadhara Pundit knew that, only to see outer appearances only of a person no one should judge him as non-devotee or non-vaishnava. It is a 'Vaishnava Aparadha' and so after the normalcy restored he told his friend Mukunda - "Dear Mukunda, I have committed a 'Vaishnava Aparadha' to respectable Sri Pundarik Vidyanidhi. Should he condone me for my fault?"

Mukunda consoled him saying - "He is a great man. Do not worry, he would not mind anything."

Sri Gadadhara, however, could not be satisfied fully by thinking that he had huge amount of 'Vaishnava Aparadha' and for this only to say 'sorry' or to seek pardoning is not sufficient. So again asked Mukunda - "I feel it is not sufficient to ask for mercy. Like a great devotee and Vaishnava he would easily condone my fault laughingly. Please for me tell him to condone me from heart strongly. Mukunda please do it."

Sri Mukunda replied - "No, if any 'Vaishnava Aparadha' committed by you, yourself should ask for mercy to him." After a pause Mukunda told Sri Gadadhara Pundit - I know you are accustomed with the worshipping of Sri Krishna but till you are not properly initiated from any devotee. You could state all the feelings and ask for mercy and thereafter, you may seek initiation from him. Perhaps you have no other alternative. Would you?"

Sri Gadadhara answered - "Oh, yes. My parents and Mahaprabhu would authorise it, I am sure. So please arrange this. Otherwise I would not get peace."

Afterwards Sri Mukunda placed the proposal of initiation to Sri Vidyanidhi. Sri Vidyanidhi then and there replied - "Oh nice, there thousands of Preceptors are available but real disciple is rare. Sri Gadadhara is one among thousands, a rare personality to find, he is also younger son of Sri Madhab Mishra and Ratnadevi who are well known to me from Chittagong. I should get an opportunity to initiate Sriman Gadadhara. It would be a great fortune for me."

Sriman Gadadhara and Sri Mukunda bowed their heads at the feet of Sri Pundarik Vidyanidhi and returned to Sribaas Angan where Sri Gouranga Mahaprabhu was engaged in Harinaam Sankirtan Mahayajna and was informed by Gadadhara all the happenings there.

Sri Gouranga Mahaprabhu - "Oh, Pundarik, 'Baap Aamar' has reached here! I was awaiting him for the last few days."

After a pause Mahaprabhu advised Sri Gadadhara to have initiation without delay because he had no much time to wait for.

Gadadhara Vaakye Prabhu Santosh Hoila,
"Shighra Karah" "Shighra Karah" Bolite Laagila.
(Ch. Bh. Madhya Chap.7)

Sri Gadadhara Pundit obeyed Sri Gouranga Mahaprabhu and did not waste time to take initiation of Radhakrishna Yugal Mantra from Sri Pundarik Vidyanidhi.

On the next day Sri Pundarik Vidyanidhi himself by walking came to Sri Gouranga Mahaprabhu and the Harinaam Sankirtan Mahayajna. It was he for whom Sri Gouranga Mahaprabhu occasionally used to call "Pundarik Baap Aamar". Now thus the Harinaam Sankirtan Mahayajna became super saturated.

Within a few days Sri Gadadhara Pundit was initiated from Sri Pundarik Vidyanidhi. And Sri Pundarik Vidyanidhi became a participant of Harinaam Sankirtan Mahayajna.

Engrossment of Lord Nrisinha

Once in the gap of Harinaam Sankirtan someone Sribaas or Gadadhara Pundit was engaged in reading the Vishnu thousand slokas:-

Yogayogabidang Neta Pradhana Purusheswarah,
Narasinha Bapuh Sriman Keshavah Purushottama. (No. 3)

With tremendous excitement of love Sri Gouranga Mahaprabhu with roaring rushed into the room of Sri Sribaas Pundit and entered where Sri Sribaas Pundit was worshipping God in the form of Nrisingha Avatara. In this shape God appeared from the wall of the palace of Demon-King

Hiranyakashipu, father of devotee Prahlad. The roaring of Sri Gouranga Mahaprabhu was the roars of a lion as God was in a shape of lion in upper part and man in lower part. Sri Sribaas Pundit hurriedly looked at Mahaprabhu and surprisingly found He was four-handed Lord Vishnu. The roaring Mahaprabhu was with conch, lotus, circle and club the four items in four hands. He realised that Sri Gouranga Mahaprabhu, Lord Vishnu, Lord Sri Krishna and Sri Nrisingha Avatara is one and the same, He is God. God can be in any shape anywhere as He feels necessary. However, Sri Sribaas was trembling for some time but having controlled himself somehow and began to read one of the verses from Sri Madbhagawata by praising Lord Sri Nrisingha Avatara.

Brhmobacha:-

Natohsmyanntay Durantashaktaye
Bichitrabiryay Pabitrakarmanye,
Bishwasy Sargasthiti Sangzaman Gunoih
Swalilaya sangddhtehbyayatmne.

Lord Brahma said - My Lord, You are unending. Your power has no limit. Your strength is of multifarious. Your deeds are sacred. With all of your the qualities you are master of all the Creation, Existences and Destruction. Yet, these activities are expressions of Your Lilas. You, however, remain having no antipathy with anything. You are the Supreme Soul. You are God.

(The Madvagawata Mahapuran by
Sri Vyasdev 7/8/40)

Sri Gouranga Mahaprabhu was thoroughly engrossed with Sri Nrisingha Avatara said to Sribaas Pundit - "Your loud Kirtan and worshipping with 'Tulsi' and water of the Ganga Narha (Sri Adwaita Acharya) máde possible of my incarnation in this world. Please do not stop of reading the verses praising me."

Sri Sribaas Pundit with folded hands sitting in front calmly requested Sri Gouranga Mahaprabhu to be pleased to see the participants and also the general people outside were waiting for the rise of their practical leader who would bring reformation to the society. And lastly, Sri Gouranga Mahaprabhu became normal as thousands of people were waiting for him.

Narasinha Aabeshe Dekhi Maha Tejomaya,
Path Chhari Vagey Lok Paiya Bara Bhoy.

(Ch.Ch. Adi, Chap.XVII)

Engrossment of Lord Shiva Mahadeva

Once, a beggar by profession singer of Lord Shiva entered into the house of Sri Gouranga Mahaprabhu. He was singing on the glory of Lord Shiva with playing with a small tabour (Dambaru) in his right hand. Sri Gouranga Mahaprabhu being engrossed with the throughts of Lord Shiva began to dance and sing with the singer. With profound excitement he jumped on the shoulder of the singer and sitting there continued the singing and dancing by jumpings. Seeing the utterly embarrassed position Sachimaa tried her best but could not. Sri Gadadhara, his constant companion, came there and politely requested him to come down. Sri Gouranga getting down gave alms to the singer so much that his bag was completely filled.

Jagai and Madhai became Vaishnava

Once, Sri Mahaprabhu had advised Sri Nityanandaprabhu and Sri Haridas to circulate Harinaam. From dawn to sunset they with singing loudly Harinaam Mahamantra began to roam on the roads and at the different houses in Nabadwip. Many of the people accepted them and started to sing Harinaam regularly and some of them denied it.

However, Sri Nityananda and Sri Haridas met two brothers Jagannath and Madhav popularly known as Jagai and Madhai. They used to pose like the 'Kotwals', the chiefs of administration of Nabadwip. They were habituated to consume liquor and remained drunk whole the days. They sitting near the 'Ghat' of the Ganga used to gossip and rebuke others in filthy words.

Originally Jagannath or Jagai was son of Raghunath and Madhav or Madhai was the son of Janardan. Both Raghunath and Janardan were the sons of rich and influential Zaminder of Nabadwip Subhananda Roy by caste Brahmin 'Kulin'. Ordinary people were being disturbed by the two cousins. There was none to dare to protest against them. The city dwellers preferred to avoid them.

One fine morning Sri Nityananda and Sri Haridas came across the notorious cousins Jagai and Madhai. Although it was morning they consumed liquor and practically as usual they lost their senses. Even they could not stare straight. Sri Nityananda and Sri Haridas while were advancing to them some of the gentlemen tried their best to forbid them cautioning not to approach them. They did not hid their ears and sang -

Bolo Krishna Bhaja Krishna Naam,
Krishna Mata Krishna Pita Krishna Dhanaprana.

(Ch. Bh. Madhya Chap.13)

The cousins had apathy in the name of Lord Krishna and so they using filthy speech were to catch the singers but failed as the singers guessing from their words the result ran towards the Sribaas Angan where Sri Gouranga Mahaprabhu was engaged in Harinaam Sankirtan Mahayajna. Jagai and Madhai at that time due to intoxication had no strength to chase them. Thus, the singers Sri Nityananda and Sri Haridas were escaped.

After a few days Sri Nityananda and Sri Haridas as per their regular daily routine were roaming and singing the song advising all the citizens in Nabadwip to sing Harinaam. Likewise at the time of return they were confronted with drunk Jagai and Madhai. They could hear the song but for the effect of intoxication could not recognize the singers. Madhai asked - "Who are you have come to disturb us in the evening?"

Sri Nityananda smartly answered - "I'm an Abadhoot, Sri Nityananda and my partner is Haridas. Would you utter the name of Lord Krishna?"

Having recognized that, these two Vaishnavas whom they earlier could not catch even after chasing, Madhai without any delay picked up a broken and emptied pot of liquor and beat it on the head of Sri Nityananda. At the second attempt of beating Jagai stopped Madhai and said to him - "What you are doing? It is not good to beat a monk. Find Madhai, it is bleeding speedily. Please stop, stop."

All bad news have high speed wings and Mahaprabhu within one or two moments received the information that Sri Nityananda is beaten by the drunken cousins. In reaction being roused Sri Gouranga Mahaprabhu along with all the participants including Sri Gadadhara Pundit and Sri Adwaita Acharya went to the spot and found Sri Nityananda was wounded and still it was bleeding. Sri Gouranga Mahaprabu did not try to control his anger but shouted as Lord Vishnu 'Chakra' and 'Chakra'. Jagai and Madhai visualised that the circle the weapon of Lord Vishnu was coming towards them. They were frightened. Sri Nityananda even with bleeding situation came forward and requested Mahaprabhu not to be angry much and reminded keep own words 'Love and only love is my religion' .

Jagai fell down at the feet of Sri Gouranga Mahaprabhu and begged for mercy. Mahaprabhu lifted him up and embraced by saying Lord Sri Krishna would see him as he did not beat Sri Nityanandaprabhu. All the associates shouted the peals of victory to Mahaprabhu. Madhai also tried to bend down at his feet to touch but Mahaprabhu denied to receive any respect from him and told him - No, no. You have to pray for mercy to Sripad Nityananda Prabhu. You have committed sin to Sripad. At first he has the right to condone your faults. Go to him and ask for mercy."

Ultimately Madhai approached Sri Nityanandaprabhu and he took him up and replied - "Alright, I have taken all your sins. But you should to take care and do not commit such sin further."

Both Jagai and Madhai were so bewildered with the behaviour of Sri Nityananda, Sri Gouranga and other associates that they fell down on the ground and fainted.

Mahaprabhu directed all others to carry the fainted Jagai and Madhai to his house, the nearest of the spot.

He also said - "Today I would give them the Mahamantra what Lord Brahma could not imagine to have".

Afterwards, the bodies of Jagai and Madhai were laid down in the courtyard of the house of Sri Gouranga Mahaprabhu. Some of the followers hurriedly arranged the sitting as Sri Adwaita in the front, Sri Gouranga Mahaprabhu in the middle, Sri Gadadhara Pundit at the left of Mahaprabhu and Sri Nityananda at the right side of Mahaprabhu. In the first row encircling Jagai and Madhai were seated Sri Pundarik Vidyanidhi, Sri Sribaas Pundit, Sri Gangadas Pundit, Sri Chandrasekhar Acharya, Sri Ramai, Sri Sriman, Sri Bakreswar Sri Banamali Acharya, Sri Suklambar Brahmachari, Sri Sridhar and other many of the associates.

Bosila Aasiya Mahaprabhu Vishwambhar,
Dui Pashe Nityananda Gadadhara,
Sanmukhe Adwaita Bosey Mahapatraraj,
Charidike Boisey Savey Vaishnava Samaj.

(Ch. Bh. Madhya Chap.13)

With the divine sound of playing 'Mridanga', 'Karatal', flute and other instruments filled the environment. Beautiful dancing and the Sankirtan started in the house of Sri Gouranga Mahaprabhu. Other inmates like Sachimaa, Vishnupriya Devi and also Sri Ishaan remained as the witnesses of the incidence.

Within a short period Jagai and Madhai regained senses and started to bow their heads to all the Vaishnavas and to cite verses praising Sri Gouranga Mahaprabhu, Sri Gadadhara Pundit, Sri Nityananda Prabhu and all other Vaishnavas.

Jai Jai Mahaprabhu Vishwambhar,
Jai Jai Nityananda Vishwambhar Dhara,

... ...

Jai Jai Adwita Jeeban Gourachandra,
Jai Jai Sahasra Badan Nityananda,
Jai Jai Gadadharapran Murari Ishwar,
Jai Haridas-Basudeva-Priyakara.

(Ch. Bh. Madhya Chap.13)

All were surprised to note that the two cousins uttered in polished language what they perhaps forgot to use for the last several years.

Jagai and Madhai became regular participants of Harinaam Sankirtan Mahayajna or Movement. They were totally changed and became real men to remember for their social services too.

After the Harinaam Sankirtan Mahaprabhu with all of them went to the Ganga in order to take baths and play in the water as Sri Gouranga Mahaprabhu preferred 'Jalakeli'.

'Bhagawatacharya's Initiation- Sri Gadadhara Pundit

A person, Sri Raghunath Upadhyay later was awarded a title 'Bhagawatacharya' by Sri Gouranga Mahaprabhu. Once in earlier time Sri Raghunath Upadhyay of Ghoranasi village of Chanduli area in the district of Bardhaman leaving everything behind settled at Baranagar on the bank of the Ganga near Kolkata proper. He after taking relief from family bondage took his worshipped 'Shalagram' stone and a copy of Srimad Bhagawata came to Baranagar. He found a solitary place at Malipara under two Neem (Margosa) trees on the bank of the Ganga. There he settled in a hut near a pond. Originally he was initially initiated in 'Shakti' mantra but loved Sri Krishna and Srimad Bhagawata.

He once knew the information of Harinaam Sankirtan Mahayajna or Movement led by Sri Gouranga Mahaprabhu. Having heard that almost all the devotees started to consider Mahaprabhu as Sri Krishna he decided to meet Sri Gouranga Mahaprabhu. On the next day at very early in the morning he began to walk towards Nabadwip alone.

At the end of the day he being tired and almost exhausted arrived at Nabadwip and found an aged man later whom he knew Sri Banamali Acharya. This man was a kind hearted and took him at Sribaas Angan. Seeing him tired and also feeling he was in need of some food Sri Sribaas hurriedly arranged necessary food for him. Afterwards he got the opportunity of seeing Sri Gouranga Mahaprabhu with his beloved Sri Gadadhara Pundit, Sri Nityananda Prabhu, Sri Adwaita Acharya, Sri Mukunda, Sri Murari,

Sri Haridas, Sri Banamali Acharya, Sri Gangadas Pundit, Sri Chandrasekhar and the other associate participants of the Sankirtan. Having been informed about his state Sri Gouranga Mahaprabhu welcomed him in the Sankirtan.

Having the opportunity to witness the Sankirtan at Sribaas Angan led by Sri Mahaprabhu in singing Harinaam and dancing with Sri Gadadhara and Sri Nityananda and also with other participants Sri Raghunath Upadhyay was overwhelmed. He at a pause fell down at the feet of Mahaprabhu and expressed his desire of having initiation in Sri Krishna mantra. Mahaprabhu advised him to take the help of Sri Gadadhara Pundit. Sri Nityananda embraced him in pleasure. Again, all resumed in the Sankirtan.

At the second pause Sri Upadhyay placed his desire praying for initiation in Krishna mantra and Mahaprabhu replied the same. Sri Nityananda again embraced him in more pleasure and said to him - "Once who loves our Sri Gouranga, he is mine and I'm of him".

At the third time, while Sri Gouranga Mahaprabhu was on the way towards the Ganga for bathing and 'Jalkeli' with all his associates Sri Upadhyay whispered - "Mahaprabhu, I like to be initiated in Krishna mantra. Please be kind to me."

Mahaprabhu in a grave voice answered not to him but ordered Sri Gadadhara Pundit - "Gadadhara, you should take him at your home and initiate him today. After the initiation he is to return to Baranagar."

Mahaprabhu also told Sri Upadhyay - "After initiation you should go back to your place Baranagar." He also assured him - "I myself would meet you there further."

According to Dr. Sukumar Sen, Sri Raghunath Upadhyay was a disciple of Sri Gadadhara Pundit. In the 'Krishnaprema Tarangini' written by Raghunath Upadhayay 'Bhakti Rasaguru Gadadhara' has been referred to:-

Dheera Shiromani Sri Gadahara Jano,
Bhagwat Acharyer Madhurasa Gaano.

(Srila Bhagwatacharyera Leela Prasanga 1st Chap. 4th Ed and 'Sripat'. By Haridas Ghosal)

Later after having Sannyas Mantra from Sri Keshav Bharti Sri Gouranga Mahaprabhu (renamed as Sri Krishna Chaitanya) on way to Puri stayed at the house of Sri Raghunath Upadhayay at Baranagar. There Sri Upadhaya had the opportunity to read the Bhagawata in front of Mahaprabhu. In reaction of the recitation and the narration of Srimad Bhagawata Mahaprabhu became so overwhelmed that he himself sang in Sankirtan and danced madly in love towards Lord Sri Krishna. The whole night was passed in Sankirtan and at the dawn of the next day Mahaprabhu greeted Sri Upadhaya declaring him as 'Bhagawatacharya'.

Eteke Tomar Naam 'Bhagawatacharya',
Ihaa Bina Aar Kono Na Kariba Karya.

(Ch. Bh. Madhya Chap.5)

III. Harinaam Sankirtan got Maturity

Laxmi Kaachh or Rukmini Sambad - Drama

Since pre-historic times acting in drama was being considered as one of the ways of educating the children and general people also. Thereafter, in Sanskrit literature a lot of dramas were written by Vaas, Kalidas and many others and probably those were also staged at different times. Still in this age of ultra modern media era drama has not lost its value in the society.

Sri Gouranga Mahaprabhu more than a half millennium year back also was well aware of the effect of dramas. In order to circulate Harinaam and to motivate all to Vaishnavism Mahaprabhu decided to stage a drama publicly to serve the purposes of Harinaam Sankirtan Mahayajna or Movement. Mahaprabhu chose a drama titled as Laxmikaachh or Rukmini Sambad. It would be spontaneous spellings by actors themselves. A three sides open stage was temporarily erected in the yard of the house of Sri Chandrasekhar and all arrangements were made by Sri Buddhimanta Khan who had adequate knowledge in stage craft, necessary costumes etc.

In the first Act after songs, as usual, sang by Sri Mukunda and afterwards his partner Sri Haridas started the recitation of prologue in the dress of a Joiner. Sri Haridas at the front of the stage introduced himself as 'Kotwal' of Baikuntha.

As 'Kotwal' he made the forecast of the events of the Act. It was pre-decided that Sri Gadadhara Pundit would act as the beautiful daughter of the King of Vidarva Vishmak. He would act in the character of the princes Rukmini.

Mahaprabhu in deep thoughts of Lord Sri Krishna could not wait for a moment and with tremendous love for Sri Krishna and excitement by wearing some of the necessary female garments appeared as Rukmini on the platform of the stage. Rukmini was writing a letter of love to Lord Krishna requesting Him to come in Vidarva and from there to take her away. Otherwise, King Shishupal whose supporter was his brother Rukmi would come and marry her. Mahaprabhu as Rukmini was writing with finger as a pen on the floor of the dais as if the surface of the earth as paper.

Mahaprabhu recollecting Lord Sri Krishna in ecstasy fainted and fell on the dais.

In this connection, we may remember the occasion of Rukmini episode in the light of 'Veerangana Kavya' in Bengali composed by Michael Madhusudan Dutta (1824 - 1973; by birth Hindu and by religion a Christian) as: -

"Aasia Garur Dhawaje, Panchajanya Naadi...
...Kaalrupe Shishupai Aasichhe Sattvare,
Aaiso Tahaar Augre.
Prabeshi E Deshe, Haro Morey.... ".

Sribaas acted on the stage in the role of Narada with grey long beard, having painted the names of Sri Krishna at twelve spots of the body and taking Vina (Lyre) hanging on one shoulder. He had one piece of 'Aasana' in hand. The spectators like Malinidevi, the wife of Sribaas, Sachimaa the mother of Mahaprabhu and others could hardly recognize the actual identity of the actor. Rather, Sachimaa became senseless with devotion to Narada for some time.

In the second Act after songs, as usual, Sri Gadadhara Pundit appeared as Laxmi or Rama in divinely dresses and ornaments with an assistant Vaishnava in the role of Suprava. There entered Brhmananda as dressed like 'Borhai', as an old woman connector or Yogamaya. Sri Haridas as Kotwal asked the three women "Where are you going?"

Borhai replied - "We are going to Mathura where Sri Krishna is living".

Sribaas as Narada asked Borhai - "Who are the two girls accompanying you?"

Brahmananda as Borhai angrily questioned - "What's your business in the matter?"

Sribaas was ashamed of and hesitatingly replied - "No, nothing, just for curiosity only."

Another actor Gangadas Pundit a senior citizen seeing night is deepening enquired - "Where you three would stay tonight?"

Having female dress Brahmananda by making a sort of fun came closer to him - "You should provide boarding facilities to us, three women. Isn't it?"

Sri Adwaitaprabhu as another joiner raising two hands up said to them - "Stop. The women unrelated and strangers are like our mothers."

Turning towards them he said - "Respected madams, you all need not feel shy. Our Lord Sri Krishna loves singing and dancing. If you can perform singing and dancing here you would get much remuneration."

On hearing Sri Adwaita, as Rama or Laxmi with make up Sri Gadadhara started to dance expressing love to Lord Sri Krishna. The stage of the drama was changed to a divine atmosphere.

Ramabeshe Naache Gadadhara Manohar,
Samaya Uchita Geet Gaya Anuchar.
Gadadhara-Nritya Dekhi Aachhe Kon Jana,
Bihbal Hoiya Nahi Karaye Krandan.
Preme Nadi Bohe Gadadharera Nayane,
Prithibi Hoiya Sikta Dhanya Hena Mane.
Gadadhara Hoila Yena Ganga Murtimati.
Satwa Satwa Gadadhara Krishnera Prakriti.
Aapane Chaitanya Boliyachhe Bar Bar,
Gadadhara Mor Baikunthera Paribaar.

(Ch. Bh. Madhya Chap.18)

Here the earlier identity in Brazalila Sri Gadadhara as Radharani could be felt by the Vaishnavas. On the stage Laxmi or Rama, as directed by Mahaprabhu, danced so nicely that all the spectators became speechless. No one of the spectators could be successful in recognizing Laxmi or Rama in original Sri Gadadhara Pundit. Sri Gadadhara had only the ambition to provide happiness to Sri Gouranga Mahaprabhu like Srimati Radharani did everything for the happiness to Lord Sri Krishna. So, the role of Sri Gadadhara Pundit was no less important than any other associates of Mahaprabhu.

All the Vaishnavas cried and shouted in the name of Hari, the Lord Sri Krishna and greeted Sri Gadadhara Pundit.

On listening to the cry Sri Mahaprabhu again entered into the stage. Sri Nityananda also appeared as a female character Borhai of Sri Mahaprabhu in the dress of Adyashakti. He was walking by bending his tall figure that could supply much pleasure to the spectators of the drama.

No one could initially understand the real form of Sri Gouranga Mahaprabhu. Some considered goddess Kamala has come. Someone thought Srimati Sitadevi has been appeared on the stage of the drama. Many of the spectators took him as Srimati Parvati, the wife of Lord Shiva

Mahadeva. Some liked to take as the Bhagirathi, the Ganga. Some as Daya and some Vaishnavas tried to guess Srimati Radharani of Varshana village of Braja has reached here on the stage. Some devotees took him as Mahamaya.

No one of the spectators could recognize Mahamaya in which character Sri Gouranga Mahaprabhu was acting. Mahamaya and Borhai i.e. Sri Gouranga and Sri Nityananda were only seen in the present scene. All the spectators were trying to understand whether Laxmi from the churning of the ocean by gods and demons altogether or the wife of Raghu Singha Sitadevi or the Mahalaxmi or Srimati Parvati, the wife of Lord Shiva Mahadeva or Vrindabaneswari the wealth of Vrindaban Srimati Radharani or the Bhagirathi or beautiful Daya or the fascinating Mohini Mahamaya who could enmesh in illusion even to Lord Shiva Mahadeva.

Sachimaa also failed to recognize her own son. She just waived her hands and folded to show due respect to the character Mahaprabhu was acting in. Sri Gouranga Mahaprabhu in order to educate the people informed all not find differences between the Strength and the Strong. No difference should be seen in Sri Krishna is the strongest and Kali-Durga-Yogamaya the mother, goddess of strength. He also advised that the strongest becomes meaningless without strength. So, everyone should offer respect to all other gods and goddesses.

Loukilk Veidic Zata Kichhu Krishnashakti,
Sobaar Sanmane Hoy Krishne Drirha Bhakti.

(Ch. Bh. Madhya Chap.18)

He looked divinely beautiful. Sri Nityananda in ecstasy became almost mad and soon fell down and fainted. All present could understand that this falling was not a part of acting. Some of the Vaishnavas hurriedly ran to him and nursed properly.

On the stage the seated on the throne divinely as Mahamayaya Sri Gouranga Mahaprabhu was being worshipped by the Vaishnavas and they, everybody present started to praise Mahamaya in respective known eulogy.

With the chanting the praising in different eulogies the night diminishes and the sun on the east was about rising. At dawn, Sri Gouranga Mahaprabhu blessed all the spectators affectionately. Before returning homes, all also bowed their heads down to Sachimaa from whom Sri Gouranga Mahaprabhu was born.

Harinaam Continues

Just after the Rukmini Sambad drama the people of the villages after villages used to gossip on the subject of Lord Sri Krishna and the Sankirtan Mahajajna or Movement. Thus, the Movement got orally publicity at different corners of the country.

Someone commented ***"Shantipur Dubu Dubu Nadia Bheshe Jay".*** This implies that in the deluge of Harinaam Sankirtan Shantipur was almost sunk and Nadia i.e. Nabadwip was being flooded in the deluge.

Sri Gouranga Mahaprabhu with all other participants and the associates used to meet every night at Sribaas Angan to perform the Sankirtan in the name of Lord Krishna. Sri Gadadhara Pundit took up the responsibility of decorating with 'Tilaka' in sandal wood paste at twelve points of the golden body of Sri Gouranga Mahaprabhu as he preferred it. He used to prepare garlands of different coloured flowers for Mahaprabhu daily. He also remained at his left side ready to supply betel leaves with some fragrant ingredients of spices from time to time in the motion of the Sankirtan. He, Sri Gadadhara Pundit had the ambition only to give pleasure to Mahaprabhu like Srimati Radharani whose ambition was only "Krishna Sukhoika Tatparya", the divine pleasure to Him and nothing else in Vrindaban. Sri Gouranga Mahaprabhu with all the participants plunged into the ocean of Harinaam Sankirtan Mahajajna almost in every night.

The other people of Nabadwip who were always in the habit of opposing Sri Krishna and Harinaam were frightened that with this movement the Rulers and their followers taking it as a part of insurrection might come up in order to subdue with enormous forces, arms and ammunitions. The Sultanate forces might not judge who have or are joining the Sankirtan or who were innocent without any touch with the Sankirtan. They would indiscriminatingly kill and destroy everything including women and religion of Nabadwip area and also other places. With this fear and also envy the people who opposed the upsurge were engaged in defaming Sankirtan and the participants thereto. These people, especially some Brahmin were also afraid of Mahaprabhu's effect on society on worshipping of many gods and goddesses with meat and liquor and thus their income and influences would come down. The considering of everyone as human being by Mahaprabhu was another issue for opposing Sankirtan and Mahaprabhu.

However the door of Sribaas Angan was kept closed for intruders. Outsiders were not allowed to enter into the Sankirtan without the permission of Mahaprabhu. Even that strict discipline if anyone enters in the Sankirtan Sri Gouranga felt that someone has entered and all the regular participants would detect the person.

Brahmin-curse as a Boon

On the way to the Ganga one Brahmin having virtuous practices but without devotion to Lord Krishna asked permission for entrance for only the fun of the Sankirtan. Sri Gouranga Mahaprabhu as he did not take interest to worship Lord Krishna declined to give him perrnission. He was so aggrieved that by tearing own sacred thread did not hesitate to curse by saying– "Your family happiness may be ruined."

Mahaprabhu's all time company Sri Gadadhara Pundit scolded him saying it was not justified to curse a divine personality like Mahaprabhu. But Mahaprabhu in himself wished to throw all the attachments from earthly materials. And so, he laughingly admitted this Brahmin-curse as a boon.

An Intruder Brahmin

One day while the Sankirtan at "Sribaas Angan" was running Sri Mahaprabhu at sometime had the feeling of uneasiness and could not find the cause behind it. He called Sribaas and requested him to verify whether any unwanted person was inside the Angan. Sribaas humbly confessed that a known pure Brahmin having virtuous practices and taking only milk has been allowed him to peruse the Harinaam Sankirtan from a hiding place. Sri Gouranga Mahaprabhu called that person in his presence and advised him only virtuous practices and taking milk is not sufficient to have the mercy of Lord Sri Krishna. Better he should devote himself to Lord.

Mother-in-law of Sribaas

In another occasion, while the Harinaam Sankirtan was in full swing Mahaprabhu again felt there was something wrong otherwise his singing and dancing in the Sankirtan could not run easily. He again called Sribaas and advised to find anything wrong there was. Sribaas started to search the wrong that happened. Lastly he discovered his own mother-in-law was listening to the Sankirtan hidingly under a cot. Sribaas brought her back and scolded her for not informing him earlier. He also cautioned not to do such hide and seek play further and devote in the worshipping of Lord Sri Krishna.

Narayani a Female Child and Sri Vrindabandas

Once, Sri Gouranga Mahaprabhu in the Sankirtan heard a cry of a child at the outside of the door. He without asking to anybody reached at the door to see who was crying. He found a female child was crying for something. It was a child Narayani only four years' old. Narayani was the daughter of Nalini, elder brother of Sribaas. After the premature death of Nalini, Sribaas brought the widow of Nalini with her child daughter to him. He looked after them at his residence at Nabadwip. Mahaprabhu sat before the child and offered the residual food what he was taking. He also advised the child not to cry again and he said - Narayani, if you want to cry, cry for Krishna and Krishna." A four years' child Narayani stopped her crying and became calm and quiet.

Later, it was known that she was married to one Baikunthadas a Brahmin (Rarhi, Chakraborty) of Natigram (Kumarhatta) near Halisahar in the district of 24 Parganas. While she was pregnant her husband suddenly died and thereafter, Sri Vrindabandas was born at the house of Sribaas at Kumarhatta probably in the year (1429 Shaka) 1507/1508 AD, Krishna Dwadashi. He remained there upto his age only five. Thereafter Basudev Dutta singer and composer of songs (like his brother Mukunda Dutta) of Mamgachhi brought the son with his mother Narayani Devi. Later, he established Sripat at Denur village of Bardhaman district. At the age of 82 in 1590 AD he breathed his last in Vrindaban.

(Prem Vilas at 24 Vilas, Vaishnava Itihas Sar Sangraha, 1st Part, p. 35, Ed. By Kishori Das Babaji)

Sri Nityanandadas wrote in Prem Vilas at 23 Vilas:-

Kumarhatta Nivasi Bipra Baikunthadas Zenho,
Tnaar Sahit Narayanir Hoilo Bibaha,
Tnaar Garve anmila Vrindabandas,
Tniho Hon Srila Vedabyaser Prakash.
Vrindabandas Zabe Aachilen Grave,
Tnaar Pita Boikunthadas Chali Gela Swarge,
Bhatrikanya Grvabati Patihina Dekhi,
Aaniya Sribaas Nija Grihe Dilo Raakhi.

(Vaishnava Itihas Sar Sangraha, 2nd Part, p. 12, Ed. By Kishori Das Babaji)

'Dukhi' to 'Sukhi'

Once, at Sribaas Angan while Sri Gouranga Mahaprabhu after the Sankirtan opted to have bath at the house instead of going to the nearer river the Ganga. Pitchers after pitchers of the water of the Ganga were brought and he used to take bath. Getting normal senses he enquired how and who brought such huge amount of water from the Ganga.

He was informed that only a maid servant 'Dukhi' by name did this job. Sri Mahaprabhu was ashtonished and told that girl - So nice your service, 'Dukhi' name is not suitable for you. You should be called as 'Sukhi'. Listen all of you from today this fortunate girl should be addressed as 'Sukhi'. Please care all of you. From then 'Dukhi" was changed as 'Sukhi'. Perhaps this fortunate girl in her later life was rewarded happiness and peace.

Chapal Gopal

In Sankirtan Mahajajna or Movement of Harinaam all remained so busy in ecstasy that could not behave with others like normal citizens of Nabadwip town. They were in touch of celestial environment in love of Lord Sri Krishna. So, the door remained closed for the night till the Sankirtan ends. The envious people who opposed the upsurge of Harinaam Sankirtan were always engaged in defaming Sankirtan and one them was Gopal Chapal.

One day, this Gopal Chapal kept on a banana leaf some materials like red flower 'Jaba', some pieces of fruits, a few pices of meat and a bottle full of liquor in order to teach the participants of the Sankirtan to worship goddess Bhabani the Sakti, the goddess of strength instead of worshipping Lord Sri Krishna.

In the morning this scene was shown to the respectable persons of the society and to Sri Gouranga Mahaprabhu. He could easily understand the miscreant's intention but remained silent with a little smile only. He thought to himself - "Alas, the miscreant does not know that the goddess of Shakti is the Yogamaya Shakti of Lord Sri Krishna. It was done by an ignorant. God would measure him." In His every action Lord Sri Krishna takes the power of Yogamaya who is the power of Lord. Even at the beginning of the Rasa Lila Lord took the assistance of Yogamaya Shakti:-

Bhagabanapi Taa Ratreeh Sharadotfulla Mallika,
Vikshya Rantung Manaschakrey Yogamayamupashrita.

(Sri Mad Bhagawata Mahapurana
by Sri Vyasdev 10/29/1)

However, the miscreant Chapal Gopal was punished for his fivorility done against the Harinaam Sankirtan. Within three days he suffered in leprosy. Understanding this and long silence of Mahaprabhu he begged for mercy from Mahaprabhu on his way daily to the Ganga. Mahaprabhu always had a smile in his lips. After a few years from Neelachal Mahaprabhu came to Fulia village and excused him and then he was cured and began to sing Harinaam sincerely.

Worshipping of Lord Vishnu by Sri Gouranga

One day, Sri Gouranga Mahaprabhu wanted to worship Sri Vishnu. Necessary arrangements were ready at Sribaas Angan by Sribaas. The devotees at the Sankirtan started to believe that Sri Gouranga Mahaprabhu was himself Lord Vishnu. So, they were eagerly looking for the 'Puja'. How it would be possible for the person who is himself Lord Vishnu. Mahaprabhu tried to worship thrice but could not as the new dresses became drenched everytime with his sweat in ecstasy of love to Lord Vishnu. Ultimately, Sri Mahaprabhu called Sri Gadadhara Pundit saying it would be better to perform the worship. The devotees at the Sankirtan were pleased to note that Sri Gadadhara Pundit who was Srimati Radharani or Srimati Laxmidevi at Vrindaban or at Baikuntha. Srimati Radharani always wanted to give pleasure to Sri Krishna likewise Sri Gadadhara Pundit had the only ambition to supply pleasure to Sri Gouranga Mahaprabhu. They nodded their heads that this arrangement of worshipping was justified.

Sheshe Gadadhara Prati Bolilen Vakya,
Tumi Krishna Pujah Mor Nahika Se Vagya.

(Ch. Bh. Madhya, Chap. 25)

Sri Gadadhara Pundit did the 'Puja' with necessary mantras. Again the participants with much more enthusiasm began to sing and dance with the instruments in the Harinaam Sankirtan encircling Sri Gouranga Mahaprabhu.

At the house of Shuklambar Brahmachari

Once Sri Gouranga Mahaprabhu wanted to have 'Prasad' at the hut of Sri Shuklambar Brahmachari. He was a beggar in profession. Once while the Harinaam Sankirtan was running in full swing Mahaprabhu from the bag swinging on the shoulder of Sri Shuklambar Brahmachari picked some handful of rice of different types as he was given by the common people of Nabadwip. He had no sense as he was dancing with Harinaam with Mahaprabhu. Some researchers like to comment that the day was of 'Ekadashi'. However, Sri Gouranga Mahaprabhu had favourable kindness to him.

There Mahaprabhu expressed his intention of taking 'Prasad' at his residence. Sri Shuklambar Brahmachari laughingly accepted the intention of Mahaprabhu. However, this made him and other associates worried for anxiety. All thought how it would be possible for Shuklambar to arrange the feast as Mahaprabhu does not take 'Prasad' alone. Many of his associates would accompany him.

On the very day surprisingly all the arrangements were complete within the proper time. Who helped or how it was possible that remained unknown to everyone even to Sri Shuklambar Brahmachari. To find the diety of Lord Sri Gopal what was not really present there Sri Gadadhara Pundit fell down and fainted. Not only Sri Gadadhara but also Sri Vijay Das, the known handwriting expert and some others were surprised to see Sri Gopal there. A pecuniary weak beggar could not establish a diety for worshipping. Yet Sri Shuklambar Brahmachari was blessed by Mahaprabhu. And ultimately, Sri Vijay Das became speechless and mad for some days. He roamed here and there.

Uthiyao Vijay Hoila Jarha Praya,
Saptadin Vramilen Sarba Nadiayay.

(Sri Sri Goudiya Vaishnava Abhidhaan (3)
by Sri Haridas Babaji p. 1200)

Murari Gupta

Murari Gupta was one of the closer companions since their studentships. He was expert in healing diseases from ailments and it was the hereditary profession. Moreover, he was a poet in Sanskrit. Later, his writing in Sanskrit on the life of Sri Gouranga Mahaprabhu and it was vastly known as 'Kadcha of Murari Gupta'. Originally he was a devotee of Sri Ramchandra.

One day, at the time of entering into Sribaas Angan Harinaam Sankirtan he showed his due respect by bending head to Mahaprabhu only. Mahprabhu having seated before the commencement of Sankirtan with Sri Nityanadaprabhu, Sri Gadadhara Pundit and other associates juniors and seniors as usual observed that without showing respect to the seniors Murari entered. He ordered him to go back home. He suggested him understand the cause and to attend Harinaam Sankirtan on the next day. Having realised Murari on the next day at first bowed to Sri Nityanadaprabhu and other seniors and then Mahaprabhu. Mahaprabhu did not say anything but smiled for a while.

This incidence was for the learning of social customs only for all the participants.

Mahaprabhu discussed his own 'Tattva' to Murari.

Kahe Prabhu Nija Tattva Murarir Sthane,
Yogaay Tambul Priya Gadadhara Bame.

(Ch.Bh. Madhya, Chap.19)

Sri Gadadhara Pundit like a living shadow of Mahaprabhu preferred to supply betel leaf to Mahaprabhu. Murari hearing the Goura Tattva became enthusiastic. He understood that Mahaprabhu Himself is the endless Universe. Then he uttered:-

Zasyoika Nihshwasita Kaalamthalmbya,
Jibanti Lomabilaja Jagadandanathah,
Vishnurmahan Sau Ihau Kalavishesho,
Givindamadipurushng Twamahang Bhajami.

(Brahma Samhita, 5/1)

Whose in single breathing time and in whose pore of the skin the owners (Brahmas) of the worlds live and Lord Vishnu is whose one 'Kala' that Govinda the Origin, Purusham I like to worship him.

On hearing this Sri Gouranga Mahaprabhu embraced Murari who was at his feet and described that he was also his life. He also expressed that he was also a devotee of Lord Sri Ramchandra and once was his friend Entellus (Hanuman).

Then Sri Gouranga showed him his four-handed shape. Murari being bewilderingly could peruse Sri Krishna of Vrindaban Lila, Sri Krishna who killed Kansa of Mathura, Sri Krishna who gave company as a friend of Arjuna in Kurukshetra, Sri Krishna who was Jadupati in Dwarka and also Sri Ramchandra who defeated Ravana and brought back Sita Maa all in Sri Gouranga Mahaprabhu. Being entranced he fell down at the feet of Mahaprabhu and said muttering - "I am the Gaurah, I am the servant for you for ever lives after lives".

One day, Sri Murari thought to himself that Sita Mata was kidnapped while Lord Sri Ramchandra existed and Lord Krishna Himself arranging the destruction of the race of Jadu and left the world by a simple arrow shot by a huntsman Jara. Then once left the Earth. He also thought if Sri Gouranga Mahaprabhu ends his 'Lila' during his own lifetime it would not be tolerated by him. So, before getting any shock furthermore he decided to finish himself. Accordingly, he brought a sharpened cutter and kept it in a hiding place in order to utilise it at night.

Sri Gouranga Mahaprabhu being competent to guess the mind of Murari again with Sri Gadadhara came to his house and wanted to see the cutter immediately. Murari was surprised to note Sri Gouranga Mahaprabhu's power to guess and brought the cutter from inside. Sri Gouranga Mahaprabhu said to him - You are not the Lord of your body. You have no right to finish the body that was looked after by your parent years after years. The society, the education centres and the teachers and the nature have made this body. Then your body is not only for yours. You have no right to finish your body. Better you give this body up to me. And think this body has been given to me for the service to mankind."

Sri Murari Gupta cried and fell down at the feet of Mahaprabhu. This Murari Gupta wrote a historical book in Sanskrit on the life of Sri Gouranga Mahaprabhu and it was vastly known as 'Kadcha of Murari Gupta'.

The Mahamantra Harinaam

One day, at Sribaas Angan Sri Gouranga Mahaprabhu in the Harinaam Sankirtan Mahajajna advised all the participants for silent and repeated recitation of the name of Sri Krishna daily as a routine:-

Hare Krishna Hare Krishna Krishna Krishna Hare Hare,
Hare Rama Hare Rama Rama Rama Hare Hare.

(Ch.Bh. Madhya, Chap.23)

He advised to chant this Mahamantra without any rules of time or numbers or the situation one falls in. Not only that, he also advised, in addition, to sing on the doors accompanying with the members of the respective families with or without any instrument but only clapping every day at evening:-

Haraye Namah Krishna Zadabaya Namah,
Gopala Govinda Rama Sri Madhusudana.

(Ch.Bh. Madhya, Chap.23)

Thus, all present having received the Mahamantra felt themselves fortunate that Mahaprabhu has taught the Harinaam to them.

Kazi Vijay

Sri Gouranga Mahaprabhu had enormous contribution for the development of the then society. He fought against casteism. He wanted to equalise all the people including the miscreants like Jagai - Madhai changed into human beings and also succeeded to regain the prestige of thousands of people in the society. He performed the historical movement against the local ruler without any weapon but by Harinaam.

Almost all the peace-loving people in Nabadwip were frightened for and also envy of the people who opposed the upsurge were engaged in defaming Sankirtan and the participants thereto. These people, especially some leading Brahmin were also afraid of Mahaprabhu's effect on society on worshipping of many gods and goddesses with meat and liquor and thus their income and influences on society would come down. The people of Nabadwip who were always in the habit of opposing Sri Krishna and Harinaam were frightened that with this movement the Rulers and their followers taking it a part of insurrection might come up in order to subdue with enormous forces, arms and ammunitions. The Sultanate forces might not judge who have or are joining the Sankirtan or who were innocent without any touch with the Sankirtan. They would indiscriminatingly kill, loot and destroy everything including women and religion by forced conversion the people of Nabadwip area and also at other places.

The considering of everyone as human being by Mahaprabhu was another issue for opposing Sankirtan and Mahaprabhu.

A few citizens mainly Brahmin and upper-class people who were frightened and whose interest and would possibly be affected by the Harinaam Sankirtan met the local Kazi the representative of the Sultanate of Bengal lodged a complaint against the Harinaam Sankirtan and Sri Gouranga Mahaprabhu. Kazi patiently listened to them. He could not reply for some time. He was previously informed by his men that those who remain engaged in the Sankirtan were not harmful for the society and also politics as Sultan Hussein Shah was on the Throne of Murshidabad the capital of whole Bengal. So, he did not feel necessary to disturb the Sankirtan of Harinaam. In the team of delegation who met him there were some influential personalities who could reach the court of Sultan Hussein Shah and could arrange whatever they desire. Many of the innocent lives might have been affected and even his chair of Kazi could be affected. After a long silence he consoled the complainers by saying that he would look after the matter later in due time.

However, the Sankirtan at Sribaas Angan was running as usual with full swing. But one day, before coming Mahaprabhu Kazi with some of his soldiers was returning from somewhere but heard the sound of Sankirtan and ordered his men to forcibly enter the Sribaas Angan. They having entered there and damaged the 'Mridanga' and other instruments and told all the participants not to continue the singing, dancing, playing instruments further. They announced that it was the order of the Kazi. They also frightened all that there awaits severe punishment for non-compliances of the order.

On return to Sribaas Angan Mahaprabhu saw the broken instruments and came to know the Ban imposed to Harinaam Sankirtan by the local Kazi. Sri Gouranga Mahaprabhu did not suppress his anger and thought that without any reaction of the imposition of unnecessary ban should not be tolerated any longer. He announced to jump into the matter immediately. All the participants of the Sankirtan should oppose the ban. With his consent on the next day thousands of participants and nonparticipants people assembled at the house of Mahaprabhu with necessary musical instruments. All were equipped with the paints of 'Tilaka' on their bodies. They also brought some handmade torches Mashals for visibility at night.

Sri Gadadhara Pundit carefully decorated Mahaprabhu with 'Tilaka' and garlands of flowers having fragrances. The fortunate people (may be our forefathers) saw fair complexioned Sri Mahaprabhu hanging two long hands, smiling face between the black hair hanging on both the sides and properly decorated. He seems to be God on this earth.

Sri Nityananda was also decorated and appeared to be Balarama who strongly can fight and sing Harinaam loudly. The others like Sri Adwaita Acharya, Sri Sribaas, Sri Gadadhara Pundit, Sri Brhama Haridas, Sri Bakreswar Pundit, Sri Murari Gupta, Sri Mukunda Dutta, Sri Nanadan Acharya, Sri Shuklambar Brahmachari, Sri Gangadas Pundit, Sri Chandrasekhar Acharya, Sri Banamali Acharya and many others were well decorated. The people who generally used to oppose Sankirtan also joined the mammoth team to register their protest against the ban on Sankirtan, the right of unarmed citizens, specially human rights.

Sri Gouranga Mahaprabhu, Sri Adwaita Acharya, Sri Gadadhara Pundit, Sri Nityanandaprabhu and many of the people of Nabadwip and its surrounding areas including physically handicapped persons also joined the team. Slowly the afternoon of the day was diminished and the night jumped on the sky. There were stars in thousands above and the torches in thousands were lit up and the place was flooded with sufficient lights. Seeing this, Sri Gouranga Mahaprabhu made some divisions of groups with singers and the players having one who would lead. All were so much disciplined to advance. He then at first with sweet but weighty voice roared - **Haribol, Haribol, Haribol"** the sound of Harinaam.

With this roaring sound it appeared that the sea Bay of Bengal was roaring nearer and coming in Nabadwip. That echoed in the thousands of voices and whole Nabadwip could hear this. As if the town Nabadwip arose from the sleep of hundreds of years from the shells of snails and came out at the first time. All there witnessed this awakening of Bengal.

Sri Gouranga Mahaprabhu, at the left Sri Gadadhara Pundit, at the right Sri Nityanandaprabhu, Sri Adwaita Acharya, Sri Sribaas, Sri Haridas and others began to move. The women of the town made the sound with their tongue 'Hulu' at a time repeatedly and blowing chonchs in order to greet the rally. They were with the dishes of paddy, grains of rice, flowers, curd, sweets, lamps lighted by 'ghee' etc for wishing them good wishes. The rally of thousands of participants was moving towards the house of Kazi at Simulia village. All the participants in the rally were so enthusiastic that there were many groups of singers and players of different musical instruments. Their singing and dancing filled the roads banks of the river the Ganga. The singers, players, devotees or non-devotees all became almost mad.

Some were singing and dancing:-

Haraye Namah Krishna Zadavaya Nemah,
Gopala Govinda Rama Sri Madhusudana.

Some of another group were singing and dancing:

Hari O Rama, Hari O Rama, Hari O Rama

One group sang with dance :-

Tuar Charane Mon Laguhure,
Sarangadhara Tuar Charane Mon Laguhure.

A group of singers and spontaneous dancer started to sing:-

Vijaya Hoila Hari - Nanada Ghosera Bala,
Hari Hari Hate Banshi Gale Banamala.

(Ch.Bh. Madhya, Chap.23)

The flow of the people with singing and dancing was completely irresistible by any power. With the roaring sound of the procession it appeared the Indian Ocean was roaring nearer to the house of Moulana Chand Kazi the administrator of Nabadwip on behalf of Sultan Hussein Shah. He heard this roaring of the rally. Although well disciplined the voluminous rally was, the people who were in the team could not find the easy way to enter the house and so, many of them had to disturb the flower garden. But all of them had to wait outside the house due to paucity of sufficient pace. Chand Kazi could not resist them and so he took shelter inside the house.

Sri Gouranga Mahaprabhu understood that Kazi hided inside the house. He sent two or three closed associates who had the fame of gentleness into the inside. Perhaps they were Sri Gadadhara Pundit, Sri Adwita Acharya and Sri Sribaas.

Bhabyaloka Pathaila Kazi Bolaila,
Bosaila Prabhu Sanman Kariya.

(Ch.Bh. Madhya, Chap.23)

They politely called Kazi and Kazi came into the sitting room where Sri Gouranga Mahaprabhu was waiting for him. Mahaprabhu showing due respect requested him to sit and himself sat on where the sitting arrangements were ready earlier. Kazi said to Mahaprabhu - "Oh, I think you're Goura! Please don't take otherwise. You with your company were aggrieved and so I went inside".

He also said - "You're son of one of the daughters of Nilambar Chakraborty. He is like my uncle in relation to our village. So, you're my nephew too. Alright, if the nephew becomes angry to maternal uncle, he should condone his fault. Moreover if the maternal uncle does any wrong to his nephew, the nephew should also take lightly his fault. Isn't it?"

Mahaprabhu admitted his explanation and showed due respect to a maternal uncle. Both of them talked for sometime. Even the Koran and the Vedas-Upanishad were discussed between them. At last, Mahaprabhu placed his complaint by saying - "The right of Sankirtan is for all, as the right of maintaining religious rites by all of all religions. This is called human right. This human right should not be banned. Isn't it?"

Kazi admitted the claim of Mahaprabhu as he also had dreamt that Nrisinha Avatara was ready to attack once. He just replied to Mahaprabhu- Alright, I and no one of my generation would stand against the Sankirtan any more. Without any harm to any of the citizens you may continue Sankirtan".

Kazi Kahe - Mor Banshe Yata Upajibe,
Tahake Talak Dibo - Kirtan Na Badhibe,

(Ch.Ch. Adi, Chap.XVII)

Sri Gouranga Mahaprabhu received the impression of the palm of Kazi an official symbol on behalf of Sultan Hussein Shah, as the Permission and Mahaprabhu addressed to the waiting people in thousands outside the room and the house by saying - "My dear devotees, my dear the citizens of Nabadwip and all of the world listen to me that Kazinama has admitted our rights of Harinaam Sankirtan. From today no one would oppose Harinaam Sankirtan further." He again in sweet but weighty voice roared - **"Haribol, Horibol, Haribol".**

All present also echoed it and began to dance in pleasure with peals of victory 'Joy Gourahari', 'Joy Gourahari', 'Joy Gourahari', 'Joy Gourahari'. They lifting two hands upward and started to return back and also began to sing Harinaam and also by singing - ***Jai Krishna Murari Mukunda Banamali - Jai Krishna Murari Mukunda Banamali - Jai Krishna Murari Mukunda Banamali*** with clappings.

They danced frantic dances like Shiva Mahadeva at various directions at their wish. They also started to sing the other songs of the Sankirtan. All the participants were advancing and Mahaprabhu with his closed associates remained at the last row. On the ways of them there were filled pitchers with banana, the leaves of mango tree at the doors of each citizen. Their houses were decorated with banana trees and garlands of different colours. All the women were also blowing chonchs and 'Hulu' and uttered - **Haribol, Horibol, Haribol"** the sound of Harinaam greeted Mahaprabhu and others enjoying their victory.

The mass led by Mahaprabhu halted at the locality of the weavers and people sang ***Jai Krishna Murari Mukunda Banamali - Jai Krishna Murari...*** Mahaprabhu sweetly smiled at them.

On the way with singing and dancing the mass found the house of Sridhar who used to sell banana leaves and stems of banana trees at the local market and Mahaprabhu would buy this cheaper vegetable from him after creating wit and fun in bargaining at laughable prices. Sometime he also used to take those loving items forcibly. But Mahaprabhu would love him and thus he was blessed.

Mahaprabhu in order to make understand his love for the devotees lifted an iron pot filled with water outside the door of Sridhar and began to drink. The pot was also broken and useless and was kept outside as a negligible utensil. Running towards Mahaprabhu Sridhar some how stopped him and assured to bring drinking water from inside the room. All other devotees observed it and they scrambled with each other to have at least one drop of the water that Mahaprabhu was able to drink one gulp only.

Louhamoy Jalapatra Bahirer Jal,
Parama Aadare Paan Koilen Sakal.
(Ch.Bh. Madhya, Chap.23)

Sridhar began to cry but Mahaprabhu and others danced and sang in joy, joy of triumph.

This indicates offering due respect to others and also to themselves. This also teaches us having respect to anybody's belief in God as God remains in everybody.

Even today if one's foot touches another's foot the people of Bengal usually bow their heads to each other. There remain no questions of casteism or other differences. This is an unwritten customs Bengal inherits after Sri Gouranga Mahaprabhu.

With the people of the mass movement Sri Mahaprabhu travelled not in Nabadwip alone but also other places like Gadigachha, Payradanga etc.

Mahaprabhu met Sarbajna Pundit whom he met in earlier occasion and showed due respect to him. He was a scholar and a hereditary Brahmin of Karnataka. He also bowed down his head and declared that Sri Gouranga Mahaprabhu is the Parama Brahma and He is the complete God.

Mahaprabhu laughingly replied to him that earlier he was in the house of Gopa, the milk man and he would play with the calves of the cows there.

This incidence of the procession and overcoming the local Kazi was the memorable for the years yet to come. Even today without any arms and ammunitions only the power of united and integrated mass can fight for the justified issues. This incidence is still a cause of inspiration for any democratic movement to establish the rights of the people of India.

A Sad Incidence

Once there was running the Harinaam Sankirtan at Sribaas Angan in full swing. Sri Gouranga Mahaprabhu was singing and dancing with others. Sri Gadadhara Pundit remained at his left side to prevent sudden falling at any time. Sri Nityanandaprabhu was also dancing on his right side in order to catch his lifelike Sri Gouranga in any emergency. But suddenly Sri Gouranga Mahaprabhu had to stop his singing and dancing as somehow he was loosing his mood. He asked Sribaas if there was anyting wrong in the house.

Sribaas took sometime to reply casually that everything was alright at Angan. But actually his only son after a few days' illness succumbed. Sribaas did not want to disturb the Sankirtan in the midway and so he cautioned all the inmates not to cry loudly and to wait for a pause of the Sankirtan. All the members including Malini Devi the mother of the deceased son restrained their outburst of mourning. They all loved Mahaprabhu so much that they did not disturb the Sankirtan.

But Mahaprabhu was aware of all the things of this Universe and he was not satisfied with the casual reply of Sribaas. He asked again - "What's the matter? Tell me Sribaas."

With the pressure of Mahaprabhu Sribaas ultimately broke into cry and expressed the incidence that happened inside the house. He also informed Mahaprabhu - "Prabhu, we cannot wait more as I think the time of funeral almost is going to be over."

Hearing this Mahaprabhu, with all the participants and associates ran to the boy and found him lying on the floor. He sat beside the boy and asked the body- You're too young, then why you are leaving your kind parent?"

It is believed by the devotees that the deceased boy replied to Mahaprabhu - "My timelimit has already expired, now let me go and leave the earth."

Mahaprabhu could not resist himself from shedding tears in pain. He was so shocked that he bagan to think all the people are binding him with personal relation 'Maya' and so he should think otherwise.

Kripa of Srimati Radharani

In Vrindaban the general people whenever meet one with another likes to address each other as **Jai Radhey.** Because without the mercy of Srimati Radharani no one gets chance to peruse the glorious feet of Lord Sri Krishna. Sri Gouranga Mahaprabhu was thoughtful of getting Lord by requesting Srimati Radharani. He believed that the mercy of the Gopis who remain with Srimati is the main key. If they are satisfied they can send a devotee to Srimati Radharani without whose permission Lord would not be available.

Mahaprabhu began to cry loudly - "Oh, my respected Gopis can you not show me the path how I can reach Srimati Radharani and my Lord?" This addressing and crying has become a regular programme of Mahaprabhu.

One day one among the students who did not like the love of Mahaprabhu for Sri Krishna sarcastically asked - "Sir, for the long time you were crying for your Krishna. But, now you are crying for the Gopis!"

Some of them volunteeringly advised him - "Leave it Sir, better you call your Krishna, it may be beneficial to you."

Krishna Naam Kene Na Lao 'Krishnanaam' Dhanya,
'Gopi Gopi' Bolile Ba Kiba Hobe Punya.

(Ch.Ch. Adi, Chap.XVII)

Sri Gouranga Mahaprabhu understood that the pupils who have less care for Lord have become much more intellectuals than necessity.

He looked at them with calmness and still eyes what the students could not tolerate nor stand and ran away.

Sri Gouranga Mahaprabhu had the strong belief that without the help of Gopis of Vrindaban no one can even desire of having Sri Krishna. Sri Krishna who for His Lila became the son of the king of Braja known as Brajendra-Nanadan and Brajendra-Nanadan is the only Lord of all.

Gopibhav Yate Prabhu Dhariyachhe Valo Mate,
Brajendra-Nanadan Mane - Aapanar Kanto.
Gopika - Bhavera Ei Sudrirha Nishchoy Brajendra-
Nanadan Bina Anyatra Na Hoy.

(Ch.Ch. Adi, Chap.XVII)

Sri Gouranga Mahaprabhu thought that the time has come to jump into the Ocean of Harinaam in the world. Mahaprabhu as usual attended the Sankirtan Mahayajna everyday at Sribaas Angan and participated in dancing and singing but always his eyes were drenched with tears. He used to cry for love of Sri Krishna. No one could stop him from crying.

Again on the Street of Nabadwip

Sri Gouranga Mahaprabhu again began to demonstrate Sankirtan on the streets of Nabadwip. He with Sri Gadadhara Pundit, Sri Nityananda-prabhu remained all the time of the day of his roaming.

Henamate Nabadwipe Prabhu Vishwambhar,
Vihare Sanhati Nityananda-Gadadhara.

(Ch.Bh. Madhya, Chap.21)

Some of the regular participants of Harinaam Sankirtan also accompanied him on several days. They were Sri Adwita Acharya, Sri Gangadas Pundit, Sri Sribaas, Sri Sriman, Sri Ramai, Sri Basudeva, Sri Jagadananda, Sri Banamali Acharya, Sri Mukunda Dutta, Sri Murari Gupta, Sri Chandrasekhar, Sri Brahmananda, Sri Govinda and many others.

Sri Gouranga Mahaprabhu himself gave Harinaam Mahamantra to the irrespective of caste and creed, poor or rich, educated or illiterate. He wanted to build an umbrella under which all could come and all could embrace each other leaving behind their own positions in the society. The silent demand of the hearts of this age was only Unity and Integrety. Mahaprabhu built this umbrella of Harinaam Sankirtan.

So, Mahaprabhu travelled on the streets and met the people of different occupations. He embraced all of them at their houses.

He believed that only Harinaam could drive yearslong frustration and would bring peace and desire of healthy living to men. At the juncture of History men should stand on their own feet with self-confidence. Without this self-confidence a man cannot stand as a man. He becomes handicapped without any strength. Any one or any miscreant can rob or loot all the belongings including wealth, health, culture, religion and also peace. Man should know himself as a man. Harinaam by any person only could unite and unity can fetch him self-confidence. So, Mahaprabhu built this umbrella of Harinaam Sankirtan.

Within a few days Mahaprabhu travelled to Nabadwip and he was successful to bring all under the umbrella of Harinaam Sankirtan Yajna i.e. Movement.

Sannyas

Having found all the people have become united Mahaprabhu decided to spread the Harinaam Movement in the country. He felt the whole country was waiting for him. He wanted to give pleasure of Harinaam to all the countrymen. He believed the beauty and the taste of Harinaam would enrich the people outside Nabadwip also.

He decided to travel in the whole country by taking Sannyas. He decided to take Sannyas. He informed Sri Nityanandaprabhu at first. Sri Nityanandaprabhu replied to him - "Your desire is the first preference. We should not oppose it."

Nityananda Bole Prabhu Tumi Ichchamoy,
Ye Tomar Ichcha Prabhu Sei Se Nishchoy.

(Ch.Bh. Madhya, Chap.25)

Sri Gouranga Mahaprabhu cautioned Sri Nityanandaprabhu this desire and the decision should not be disclosed to anybody. Sri Gouranga Mahaprabhu went to Sri Mukunda Dutta and heard the songs sang by him. Afterwards he expressed his desire of taking Sannyas to Sri Mukunda who became depressed. However, he believed that Mahaprabhu is himself God and so no arguments would act. He was crying and keeping him in crying position Mahaprabhu then met Sri Gadadhara Pundit.

Sri Gadadhara Pundit seeing Mahaprabhu in his front he felt fortunate that God has appeared to him. Accordingly he welcomed him.

Sambhrame Charane Bandilen Gadadhara,
Prabhu Bole, Shuno Kichhu Aamara Uttar,
Na Rahibo Gadadhara Aami Grihabaase,
Ye Te Dige Chaliibang Krishnera Uddeshe.
Shikha Sutra Aami Sarbathaya Na Rakhibo,
Matha Mundaiya Ye Te Deshere Chalibo.

(Ch.Bh. Madhya, Chap.25)

Sri Gouranga Mahaprabhu would shave his tuft and all the hair at the time of taking Sannyas. This was a painful matter for the thousands of devotees of Harinaam Sankirtan. They were habituated to have darshan of Mahaprabhu with curled black hair on his head and hanging on the both sides of his shoulders. The people would like to see the divine beauty of their most respected and favourite Mahaprabhu. If he takes Sannyas his appearance would be changed.

Sri Gadadhara Pundit, however, could not guess this decision earlier so to him it seemed like a bold in the blue sky. He thought how Sachimaa and Vishnupriyadevi would survive without Sri Gouranga? They may not be able to cope with this shock of his departure. They would become helpless.

Ultimately Sri Gadadhara Pundit also thought that Sri Nemai has taken decision obviously having judged it in every respect so others should not be worried.

He informed the matter to only six persons Sri Nityananda, Sri Gadadhara Pundit, Sri Mukunda, Sri Brahmananda, Sri Govinda and Sri Chandrasekhar and above all, he sought for approval of Sachimaa and cautioned all of them not to disclose the matter earlier before his departure. Haridas perhaps could get it seeing Sri Gadadhara Pundit and Sri Nityananda so sad.

Sri Gouranga Mahaprabhu at first tried to console Sachimaa. She could not tolerate this information that her son would be a Sannyasi. She fainted repeatedly. She also asked if Mahaprabhu leaves his mother and wife Vishnupriya behind how could she explain to other domestic persons who run their families together with old aged parent, wife and own children? This is the religion of any domestic person is not to leave any of them for own pleasure and happiness.

Sri Gouranga Mahaprabhu consoled Sachimaa saying that she was his mother in all the ages while God was incarnated. He cited the examples of Bamana Avatara and mother Aditi, Kapil Muni and Devahuti, Sri Ramchandra and mother Koushalya, Krishna and mother Devaki. He also assured to be her son in the forthcoming ages also. Hearing this Sachimaa somehow could control herself for the time being.

In the evening Sri Nemai went to the 'Ghat' of the Ganga and bowed head towards the Ganga and therafter returned home and sat there with his associates like Sri Gadadhara Pundit, Sri Nityanandaprabhu and others. Thousands of devotees with garlands and sandalwood paste assembled the house and sat before Mahaprabhu. Mahaprabhu greeted all the devotees by giving all the garlands from his neck. Sri Gouranga advised them to sing the Lord's name as:-

Bolo Krishna Gao Krishna Bhajo Krishnanaam,
Krishna Binu Keha Kichu Na Bhabiba Aan.

He again advised them:-

Ki Shayane Ki Bhojane Kiba Jagarane
Aharnishi Chinta Krishna Balaha Badane.

(Ch.Bh. Madhya, Chap.26)

All of them began to sing Lord's name and after sometime participated in dances as they used to do in 'Sribaas Angan' and all of them received 'Prasad' with full satisfaction.

During this period Sridhar brought a gift a piece of bottle gourd from his house. Mahaprabhu thought it might not come into his use because he would not see the next daylight in Nabadwip as it was his last night there.

Like other normal days another devotee brought some milk for Mahaprabhu as gift. He requested Sachimaa to cook the bottle gourd in milk at this night. Sachimaa having been pleased went to the kitchen for cooking bottle gourd with milk and offered to her only and loving son

Sri Nemai who at the night was to adieu to family life in order to enter into the life without any bondage.

At night Sri Gadadhara Pundit and Sri Haridas lied down on the portico outside the bed-room of Mahaprabhu. For anxiety they almost remained sleepless the whole night. Before the dawn Sri Gouranaga Mahaprabhu rose from the bed and came out to set for the journey.

Seeing Sri Gouranga outside the room Sri Gadadhara and Sri Haridas stood up and with folded hands requested him - "We may accompany you."

Gadadhara Haridas Uthilen Jani,
Gadadhara Bolen Chalibo Sange Aami.

(Ch.Bh. Madhya, Chap.26)

Sri Gouranga Mahaprabhu replied - "No, not now. I am going to Katowa and there Sri Keshav Bharati is waiting for me."

After passing sleepless night Sachimaa also was waiting for her Nemai. She was crying silently. She could not cry loudly if the neighbourers and Srimati Vishnupriya would wake up.

Jananira Padadhuli Loi Shire,
Pradakshin Kori Tnaare Chalila Sattware.

(Ch.Bh. Madhya, Chap.26)

Sri Gouranga Mahaprabhu touched the feet of the mother Sachidevi. Having got the silent blessings from the mother Sri Gouranga Mahaprabhu started for the journey on foot towards the 'Ghat', now named as 'Nidaya Ghat' of the Ganga.

On the next day morning Sachimaa the 'Jagat Janani' burst into tears and cried loudly what aches the hearts of Vishnupriyadevi and all the neighbourers. Thousands of the devotees and also non-devotees assembled at the courtyard of Sachimaa's house. All were tremendously shocked. It appeared to be intolerable to them.

At Katowa, on the next day Sri Gadadhara Pundit, Sri Nityananda, Sri Mukunda, Sri Chandrasekhar Acarya, Sri Brahmananda probably Sri Haridas and many other devotees to whom these people could not conceal and accompanied from the 'Ghat' assembled at the Sripat of Keshav Bharati.

Sri Gouranga Mahaprabhu bowed his head at the feet of Keshav Bharati and praised him by saying - "Please, keep mercy on me. You are a lovely great merciful man. Lord Sri Krishna lives in you. You are the only person who can co-operate me to take Sannyas in order to roam all the places for love of Sri Krishna. Please do not try to refuse me. Please do not avoid me. I am here to take the Sannyas Mantra so that I can serve Lord Sri Krishna."

The whole day Sri Gouranga Mahaprabhu passed all the time in discussion on Lord Sri Krishna and His divine activities with all who were present.

The hundreds of people from Katowa also assembled there to find a Brahmin youth from Nabadwip who made many people attracted to Harinaam has left family Iife and decided to take Sannyas. Many of the people were crying in shock to see a Brahmin youth of only 24 years' of age leaving family life was going to take Sannyas from Keshav Bharati.

On the next day the 2nd Magh of 1431 Shaka (16th or 17th January 1510 AD) Sri Chandrasekhar Acarya aged maternal uncle arranged all the materials for the rites of taking Sannyas.

The barber having profession of hair cutting and shaving named Madhu or Haridas with drenched eyes and slow motion took his seat nearer to the 'Ghat' of the Ganga and Sri Gouranga also sat there in his front for shaving purpose.

There were hundreds of spectators and devotees from Katowa and of adjacent areas including the associates from Nabadwip assembled encircling Sri Gouranga Mahaprabhu. They somehow controlled their tears from sheddings. Many of them began to cry despite their efforts of controlling. The barber remained inactive with the cutting apparatus razors and scissors for sometime but lovely Nemai Pundit advised him to make haste.

Amongst the cries of hundreds in shock lastly Madhu cut at first the tuft what indicated the identity of a Brahmin. Nemai Pundit known as Sri Gouranga Mahaprabhu was very much pleased that his identity as Brahmin would no more to become an obstacle for the thousands of the people of various castes and creeds. His movement was to unite all irrespective of any difference between men and him. He thought, for this revolutionary endevour the umbrella of Harinaam would be more successful in the society.

With also the tears in eyes Sri Keshab Bharati at last gave the mantra in the ears of Sri Gouranga Mahaprabhu and thus Sri Gouranga was initiated in Sannyas Mantra and also was named by Keshab Bharati as **Sri Krishnachaitanya** as all the persons who came in contact Harinaam led by Sri Gouranga Mahaprabhu got consciousness of Lord Sri Krishna. Mahaprabhu has enlightened the people irrespective of all differences with the consciousness of Lord Sri Krishna through the Harinaam Movement.

Most of the devotees were also believed that Sri Gouranga Mahaprabhu was himself Lord Sri Krishna. Many people of the crowd were also convinced that the name **Sri Krishnachaitanya** was justified. All the people assembled started to sing Harinaam loudly and danced encircling Mahaprabhu **Sri Krishnachaitanya** for a long time.

After the initiation Sri Krishnachaitanya Mahaprabhu began to run towards the west direction to reach Vrindaban where Lord Sri Krishna has performed His Lilas with the Braja Gopis and Srimati Radharani. He was then engrossed with the love of Lord Sri Krishna. He was not in practical sense that to reach Mathura Vrindaban it would take more than two months by walking only. He had no other necessary preparation of journey nor decided who would accompany him.

With him all the associates including the Preceptor Keshab Bharati also followed running Sri Krishnachaitanya Mahaprabhu and no one could realise the intention.

Nityananda Gadadhar Mukunda Sanhati,
Gobinda Pashchate Agre Keshab Varati.

(Ch.Bh. Madhya, Chap.14)

Sri Krishnachaitanyadev was charmed with the scenes of various colour of flowers that blossom in the spring at this *rarh* area of Bengal but he did not find anyone who utters Harinaam. Without Harinaam a place there, he also desired to die in a nearby pond in shock of not uttering Harinaam. All of the followers wanted to stop him but couldn't. At last one of them could overtake running Sri Mahaprabhu Krishnachaitanya and tried to divert the direction of his running. Sri Nityananda arranged some of the boys who were playing with the cows and calves on the ground to utter at least one Harinaam. They suddenly shouted "Hari, Hari Bola' what poured the honey in the ears of Sri Krishnachaitanya Mahaprabhu. He stopped there nearer to Bakreswar and left the desire of suicide and accompanied the followers towards the east where the river Ganga flows towards the sea Bay of Bengal. He was understood that Sri Sri Jagannath Mahaprava of Neelachal was calling him and so, after bathing in the Ganga it would be better to go to Puri.

Bahya Prakashiya Prabhu Nija Kutuhale,
Bolite LagiloChalilam Neelachale,
Jagannathaprabhura Aajna Hoilo More,
Neelachale Tumi Jhat Aaiso Sattware.

Eto Boli Chalilen Hoi Purbamukh,
Bhakta Sob Paailen Parananda Sukh.

(Ch.Ch. 3rd and Antya, Chap.l)

The team returned at the bank of the Ganga. He advised Sri Nityananda to meet Sri Adwaita Acharya at Shantipur first and then to Nabadwip to inform Sri Sribaas Pundit and others who could not guess the initiation in Sannyas Mantra. He also requested Sri Nityananda to arrange to bring Sachimaa at the house of Sri Adwaita Acharya and he would go to Phulia village of Haridas and afterwards return to Shantipur.

On the next day while bathing in the Ganga just opposite of Shantipur Sri Krishnachaitanya Mahaprabhu praised the glory of the Ganga and he also felt that he was bathing in water of the Yamuna and praised the Yamuna by saying:-

Chidanando Bhanoh Sadananda Sunoh Paramo Premagatri
Draba Brhmagatri,
Aghanang Lavitri Jagatkshemadhatri Pabitri Kriyanno
Bapurmitraputri.

Sri Nanada Nandan's loving body of diluted Brahma of what abolishes the sins and works for the good of all the river Kalindinandini may please pure my body.

(Sri Sri Leelamadhuri by Rasikmohan Vidyanidhi)

Sri Adwaita Acharya at Shantipur

Then Sri Krishnachaitanya Mahaprabhu was welcomed by Sri Adwaita Acharya with new dresses like loin-cloth and outer cloth a boat for returning to Shantipur. There Sachimaa was brought by a palanquin by Sri Nityanandaprabhu and assembled the other thousands of devotees from Nabadwip and from adjacent areas.

All of them at the first sight of shaved Mahaprabhu with dress of an ascetic got much shock. However, Sachimaa who did not receive any food and remained in fasting for the last twelve days entered into the kitchen of Srimati Sitadevi and Srimati Shreedevi the two wives of Sri Adwaita Acharya in order to prepare palatable dishes for her only son and his associates.

All the devotees after lamentation began to sing the songs liked by Mahaprabhu.

Here Sri Krishnachaitanya Mahaprabhu repeatedly confessed to mother Sachidevi that never he would be able to pay up the debts of his mother in life.

At Shantipur, Sri Krishnachaitanya Mahaprabhu remained at the house of Sri Adwaita Acharya for ten days. There were more than sufficient arrangements of cooking for offering to Sri Sri Radha Madana Gopal, the deities established by Sri Adwaita Acharya. All were engaged in Sankirtan. There were Sri Sribaas, Sri Ramai Pundit, Sri Pundarik Vidyanidhi, Sri Gangadas Pundit, Sri Chandrasekhar Acharya, Sri Bakreswar Pundit, Sri Murari, Sri Shuklambar Brahamachari, Sri Buddhimanta Khan, Sri Nandan Acharya, Sri Sridhar, Sri Vijoy, Sri Basudeva Dutta, Sri Damodar Pundit, Sri Sanjoy, Sri Mukunda Dutta, Sri Gadadhar Pundit and Sri Nityanadaprabhu and many others fortunate devotees and they made the house of Sri Adwaita Acharya as 'Boikuntha'.

At last, although Sachimaa requested her Nemai would settle nearer, after the long discussions it was decided that Sri Nemai i.e. Sri Krishnachaitanya Mahaprabhu would go to Neelachal and Sachimaa admitted it:-

Tate Ei Yukti Valo Mor Mone Loy,
Neelachale Rahe Yadi Dui Karya Hoi,
Neelachale Nabadwipe Yena Dui Ghar,
Lok Gatagati - Barta Pabo Nirantar.

(Ch.Ch . Madhya, Chap.III)

IV. On Way to Neelachal

From Shantipur

Mahaprabhu set for Neelachal on foot. Sri Gadadhar Pundit, Sri Nityananda, Sri Mukunda, Sri Jagadananda, Sri Brahmananda and Sri Govinda accompanied him.

Nityananda Gadadhara Mukunda Govinda,
Samhati Jagadananda, Aar Brhmananda.

(Ch.Bh. Antya, Chap.1)

Mahaprabhu started to walk on foot along the east side of the river Ganga and reached Atisara, Andhamuni in the area of South 24 Parganas district as the mainstream of the Ganga then used to flow through this area before entering into the Bay of Bengal.

At Atisara

At Atisara, he with his associates accepted the alms at the house of Ananta Pundit. Mahaprabhu praised the devotion of Ananta Pundit.

At Chhatrabhog

At Chhatrabhog, the people of the villages welcomed the whole team. They were much happy to have darshan of Mahaprabhu and the associates. There remains the deity of Lord Shiva known as Ambulinga under water. He visited Shiva Mahadeva there. He also became pleased to find the hundred branches of the Ganga towards the Bay of Bengal. With absorption in thought of Lord Sri Krishna his feet slipped and nearer Gadadhara Pundit and Sri Nityanandaprabhu held in hands and thus escaped from falling. Sri Nityanandaprabhu took him in his broadened lap. All of the associates began to sing Harinaam and danced.

Service of Ramchandra Khan

A great zaminder Ramchandra Khan, one of the heredity of Sri Gunaraj Khan, there came forward and helped Mahaprabhu by arranging a boat and trusted sailor to take of them at night to Odisha ruled by a Hindu Raja Pratap Rudra.

It was then war-time in between Hussein Shah of Goud Bengal and Raja Pratap Rudra of Odisha-Kalinga area. So there were possibilities of any danger like looting others' property and also lives by dacoits in the water and boarder guards on the soils at different borders. Not only that there were Royal Bengal Tiger in the forest on the banks. Mahaprabhu knew only Lord Sri Krishna who can save if He desires.

After boarding in the boat the associates began to sing Kirtan with their Mridanga and other available instruments. But the sailor was afraid of any occurrence by the miscreants in water as their remains no rule of any administration in water. So he requested to stop their Kirtan or any other sound.

Eteke yabt Odra Deshe Nahi Pai,
Tabat Nirab Hao Sakal Gossain.

(Ch.Bh, Anlya, Cha p.2)

At Prayag Ghat

Mahaprabhu reached at Prayag Ghat and bathed there with all his associates. Here he went to a temple and bowed his head to the deity of Shiva Mahadeva known as established by Yudhisthira in the age of the Mahabharata.

He then let other associates to wait at a place of temple area and went out in the villages to collect alms for all of them. The villagers to see the young ascetic with divine look were surprised and they tried their best to give alms as good as they could. After return from begging handed all the materials over to Jagadananda for the arrangement of cooking.

Afterwards on the road through forest area the team was forbidden to enter the local area border by a certain watchman. He demanded necessary entry tax from the persons of the team. The tax collector having found Sri Gouranga an ascetic allowed only him to cross the border. Mahapabhu having crossed the border sat under a tree nearer to the border and started to take in mind the name of Lord Sri Krishna and automatically tears from his eyes were flowing.

The other persons of the team requested the tax collector by saying that they were with this ascetic. Seeing them in different dresses the tax collector did not believe them. However, returning to Mahaprabhu asked whether the other persons belonged to him. Mahaprabhu sarcastically replied- "All in this Universe have separate entities, everybody is linked with others. Then there does not exist who is belonged to me or to whom I am belonged."

So, the tax collector again demanded the necessary entry fees to them who were awaiting beyond the border. The associates understood that he could not apprehend what Mahaprabhu answered. They again requested him earnestly to say to Mahaprabhu specifically.

Being much annoyed the tax collector again reached the spot where Mahaprabhu was in deep meditation and the base of the tree was drenched with sufficient water that was flowing incessantly from his eyes. He was surprised to note the amount of tears that were flowing.

Dani Bole E Purush Nara Kabhu Nahe,
Manushyera Nayane Ki Eto Dhara Bohe.

(Ch.Bh. Antya, Chap.2)

The tax collector generally knows nothing but collection of money legal or illegal yet he is a man with his heart where remains soft corner. He again slowly came to the persons of the team and said - "He is crying much with his eyes shut up. Please tell me the truth".

One of the associates replied - "We are from Goud Bengal. He is Sri Krishnachaitanya Mahaprabhu our Sri Gouranga. He has taken Sannyas recently and all of us going to Puri to have darshan of Lord Sri Sri Jagannathswami."

The tax collector with his eyes drenched too allowed all of them and bowed his head to Mahaprabhu and them. He also begged mercy by saying -

Aparadha Kshama Karo Karunasagar,
Chalo Neelachal Giya Dekhaha Sattwara.

(Ch.Bh, Antya, Chap.2)

Nityananda Broke the Stick

Sri Jagadananda was carrying the stick as one of the signs of ascetic of Sri Krishnachaitanya Mahaprabhu. He was always in search of any temple old or new where he would reach. After the bathing in the water of the Subarnarekha he with Sri Gadadhara Pundit, Sri Mukunda, Sri Govinda and Brahmananda entered the villages to find temples. He had advised

Sri Nityananda and Sri Jagadananda to wait at the bank of the river Subarnarekha.

Sometime later Jagadananda seeing late of returning of Mahaprabhu and others thought it was sure that Mahaprabhu was engaged in singing and dancing at some temple and forgot to return to the riverside. Perhaps his associates could not dare to remind him to return. He requested Sri Nityananda to hold the stick of Mahaprabhu and entered the nearer village to have some alms for cooking for the day.

Sri Nityananda holding the stick sitting on the bank of the river Subarnarekha (Vargi) looked at it and said to himself - "Oh, my dear Stick it would not be wise that Mahaprabhu would carry you while I myself carry him always in my heart."

Ahe Danda Aami Jare Bahiye Hridaye,
Se Tomare Bahiben Eto Yukta Nahe,
Eta Boli Balarama Prarama Prachanda,
Felilen Dandwa Bhangi Kari Tina Khanda.

(Ch.Bh. Antya, Chap.2 and
Ch. Ch.Madhya, Chap V)

Sri Nityananda did not want that Mahaprabhu would carry a stick to show his identity as an ascetic. He broke the stick in three pieces and threw at some distance.

Having returned Jagadananda found the stick was broken by Sri Nityanandaprabhu. On return of Mahaprabhu being informed laughed and asked Sri Nityanandaprabhu - "Sripad, if God resides in everything He also remains in the stick. I cannot understand what wrong has been done by it. Alright, what happened that was the desire of Lord Sri Krishna."

Mahaprabhu consoled himself that at least one belonging is left what would be better for a Sannyasi who has left everything behind for the life.

At Remuna

Sri Krishnachaitanya Mahaprabhu with all the associates visited the Jaleswar Shiva Mahadeva and thereafter reached Remuna where the diety of Gopinath remains.

According to a legend this Gopinath was known as Kshirchora Gopinath and the deity Himself stole a pot of Kshir, a tasty item of sweets prepared by condensing milk for the most pioneer Vaishnava Sripad Madhabendra Puri who lived on volunteering alms only.

For the whole day for not asking any alms to anybody remained foodless and so was feeling also hungry in the evening. On the other hand, the priest of the temple offered twelve earthen pots of Kshir and after greeting with waving lamps, fans etc. to the deity and afterwards arranging the prasads for recipients found one of the pots was missing. He generally thought that at the time of setting one pot might have been mistaken by him. He locked the door for the night and went to sleep at his residence.

At night the priest dreamt that the deity of Lord Gopinath Himself kept aside one of the pots of Kshira behind for His devotee unfed pioneer Vaishnava Sripad Madhabendra Puri. He woke up and ran to the temple and with great surprise found the missing pot at the backside of the deity.

Having taken the pot the priest came out of the temple and began to search for the unfed Vaishnava. It was deep night and there it also rained in small drops. At that time Sripad Madhabendra Puri was remembering Lord's name sitting under an almost torn canopy where weekend markets were run. At last the priest found the Vaishnava there and said cryingly in love of Lord - "Gossainji, you are here! See Lord Gopinath is so merciful that He Himself has kept one pot of Kshira for you. Please receive the Prasada and appease your hunger."

Sripad Madhabendra Puri was astonished to find the pot of Kshira and with eagerness and respect received it from the hands of the priest. Remembering Lord he ate the contents and afterwards broke the emptied earthen pot and kept all the pieces in the cloth that usually hangs on his side while moving. Both the Vaishnava and the priest began to sing the glory of Lord Gopinath as well as Lord Sri Krishna.

Sri Krishnachaitanyadeva remembered the episode and cried for Lord's kripa on Sripad Madhabendra Puri for some time and afterwards he with other associates began the Sankirtan by singing and dancing with enthusiasm. The whole place turned into a celestial environment.

Sri Krishnachaitanyadeva was informed that this deity of Lord Gopinath once was established by Uddhaba whom Lord Sri Krishna from Mathura sent to Braja to find how mother Jashoda and father Nanda were passing their days. He also requested Uddhaba to meet the Sakhis and their Vrindabaneswari Radharani to find how they were living without Sri Krishna there. His feelings that were discussed in the Srimad Bhagwata by Sri Vyasdeva and from there a nice 'Bhramar Gita' was found.

At Jajpur

Sri Krishnachaitanya Mahaprabhu visited the whole day at Jajpur. The place had innumerable temples of various deities of gods and goddesses from ancient times. He sang and danced everywhere in love of Lord Sri Krishna. He also sang and danced where Shiva Mahadeva and mother Shaktidevi found. All the local people were surprised to note it and many of them also participated in the Sankirtan.

Shakshi Gopal at Cuttack

Sri Chaitanyadeva after bathing in the water of the river Mahanadi visited the temple at Sakshi Gopal at Cuttack and with all the associates sang with nicely dancing there. He was highly appreciated and all the local people greeted him with much enthusiasm.

At Bhubaneswar

Thereafter reached Bhubaneswar and the temple where Shiva Mahadeva exists for long time near the Bindu Sarobar full of water brought from many pilgrimages. It is told that this place is the secret Kashidham, the residence of Shiva Mahadeva.

Mahaprabhu bathed in the water of Bindu Sarobar. He advised all his associates to obey Lord Shiva Mahadeva. In the Bhagawata Lord Shiva Mahadeva has been considered as **"Vaishnavanang Yatha Shambhu".**

Shiva Rama Govinda Boliya Gourroy,
Hathe Tali Diya Nritya Karen Aadaya.

(Ch.Bh, Antya, Chap.2)

Mahaprabhu had been at all the temples of Shiva or Kali or Krishna and there he sang and danced with enthusiasm. Many local people became surprised and were inclined to the Philosophy of Mahaprabhu "Samattwang". He was cordially received by all the people where he reached, sang and danced.

Seisob Grame Prabhu Bhaktavrinda Sange,
Shivalinga Dekhi Dekhi Bhramilen Range,
Parama Nivrita Ek Dekhi Shivasthan,
Sukhi Hoilo Sri Gourasundar Bhagawan.

(Ch.Bh. Antya, Chap.2)

We can cite that the great poet Joyadeva who was a poet in the court of Raja Laxman Sen of Bengal (in 12th century) and wrote the '*Geeta Govinda*' was also a priest at Kusheshwar Shiva on the bank of the river Ajoy in the Kenduli village of Birbhum.

At Kamalpur

Sri Chaitanyadeva reached Kamalpur. From here the flag on the top of the main temple is visible. Seeing this flag he became so happy and embraced his associates with joy. He has seen the flag and the circle on the top of the temple. With the love and respect to Lord Jagannatha he became overwhelmed. Now the journey of the long path is being finished. He and all his associates felt divine joy in their hearts. And it was a natural thing.

Deulera Dhwaja Matra Dekhilen Dure
Prabeshila Prabhu Nija Aananada Sagare.

(Ch.Bh . Antya, Chap.2)

At Atharonala

Sri Chaitanyadeva with all the associates arrived at Aatharonala (the eighteen streams) and saw the pinnacle of the temple of Lord Jagannatha. With folded hands he bowed his head and becoming in normal state thanked in gratitude to all the associates "Friends, thank you all for giving me valuable company, guidance and helping time to time. Now tell me, whether I should run towards the temple first keeping you behind or anyone of you like to go first?"

Sri Gadadhar Pundit, Sri Nityanandaprabhu, Sri Govinda, Sri Brahmananda and Sri Jagadananda remained silent. On behalf of them only Sri Mukunda replied to him - "Better you proceed forward. We cannot compete with you in racing you know. We are coming in our normal speed by following you."

V. Neelachal Leela 1

"Jagannathaswami Nayana Pathagami Bhabatu Me...

The Neelachal Leela of Sri Chaitanyadeva begins. It was day time and a time of morning 'Bhog' of Sri Sri Jagannathadeva, Sri Sri Balaramadeva and Srimati Subhdradevi inside the sanctum of the temple.

But with profound emotion for love of Sri Krishna as well as Sri Sri Jagannathadeva Sri Chaitanyadeva without caring anything left or right rushed towards the deities straight and suddenly slipped his leg and fell down on the floor.

There were guards on duty to see lest anyone could cross the markings and enters the reserved area of the main hall for Lord's 'Bhog'. The three or four guards on duty noticed him falling and they with lifting their canes and considering an intruder ran to him, perhaps two or three strikes were beaten. Hurriedly Rajpundit Sri Sarbabhoum Bhattacharya, who luckily was present there, came forward and saved by placing own back covering the unknown young ascetic. He was highly respected by many of the guards and the royal people in the temple.

It was probably in the month of Falguna of 1431 Shaka (1510 AD) when Sri Chaitanyadeva reached Neelachal.

Rajpundit Sri Sarbabhoum Bhattacharya was not familiar person to Sri Chaitanyadeva but he saved him in humanitarian grounds covering by his back on the body of the young ascetic only by seeing deep devotion for Lord Jagannathadeva.

Ajna Parihari Sob Uthilo Marite,
Aaste Byaste Sarbabhoum Padila Prishthete.

(Ch.Ch. Madhya, Chap V)

He was also attracted to the young ascetic having shaved head and wearing saffron outer dresses. However, he arranged with his loyal and trusted men to take the fainted ascetic at his own residence.

Thus, the experience of first day was of Sri Chaitanyadeva in Puri (Neelachal). It may be presumed the day was a few days back of Dolyatra in the month of Falguna of 1431 Shaka (1510 AD).

Sri Sarbabhoum

The other associates of Sri Chaitanyadeva like Sri Gadadhar Pundit, Sri Nityanandaprabhu, Sri Govinda, Sri Brahmananda, Sri Jagadananda and Sri Mukunda arrived at the temple but could not initially find their beloved Sri Chaitanyadeva. They were some later informed that Rajpundit Sri Sarbabhoum Bhattacharya arranged with his loyal and trusted men to take the fainted ascetic at his own residence. With the help of a near relative of Sri Sababhouma Bhattacharya they were taken at the house where Sri Chaitanyadeva received shelter.

Prabhu Bole Jagannatha Barah Kripamoya,
Aanilen More Sarbabhoumera Aalaya.
(Ch.Bh, Antya, Chap.2)

After a few days' stayal at the house of Rajpundit Sri Sarbabhoum Bhattacharya by Sri Chaitanyadeva, Sri Sarbabhoum who was an eminent teacher of the Vedanta knew the actual identity of the 24 years' young monk Sri Chaitanyadeva was earlier known the son of Sri Jagannatha Mishra. He then decided to coach him the lessons from the Vedanta and Sri Chaitanyadeva agreed to attend the classes. He was always a serious and sincere student began to take classes. He listened to the class for uninterrupted seven days without any question. Sri Sarbabhoum noticed minutely the silence of his new student. Ultimately he asked whether there was any difficulty in accepting the lessons in the classes.

Sri Krishnachaitanyadeva replied that everything he had listened to Sri Sarbabhoum. He easily explained the theory of Brahma, the 'Ekamebadwitiyam' and the theory of devotion to God. He also said that there in the lessons remained the absence of 'Bhakti' the devotion to Lord Sri Krishna. Without the discussion of 'Bhakti' all learnings were tasted insipid to him. Sri Sarbabhoum Bhattacharya was surprised and finally he could realise that the young boy, the son of Jagannatha Mishra of Nabadwip was not an ordinary man. He was more than what he thought once. He began to determine the actual identity of his new student.

After a pause Sri Sarbabhoum looked at Sri Chaitanyadeva and found the 'Shadabhuja Murti' instead of Sri Chaitanyadeva there. Sri Sarbabhoum found him with six handed appearance. To see this 'Shadabhuja Murti' he recognized him as God and bowed his head and soon fainted.

Sri Chaitanyadeva afterwards cautioned him not to disclose what he witnessed. But he could not forget the appearance of God. It is believed that the painting as 'Shadabhuja Murti' on the inside wall of the temple of Lord Jagannatha Mahaprabhu as he witnessed was done by Sri Sarbabhoum Bhattacharya.

However, Sri Krishnachaitanyadeva decided perhaps Lord Jagannatha-deva desires that he should have darshan of Lord Jagannathaswami with Sri Balarama and Srimati Subhadra Devi regularly by standing only at the Gadurh Pillar and it continued for the whole tenure. His devotion and love for Lord was so deep that all the time his eyes would flow tears. The accumulation of tears on a piece of stone on which he used to stand by the side of the Gadurh Pillar once was eroded.

Later, many of the visitors at the temple including Swami Vivekananda were surprised to note such the depth of emotion and love for God as he had.

(Complete Works - Centenary Volume - VI)

Sri Chaitanyadeva Discovered the Deity of Gopinath

One fine afternoon Sri Krishnachaitanyadeva with all the associates including some devotees of Odisha was seated on the sands of the sea beach. They were talking on Lord Sri Krishna and Lord Jagannatha. There was the vast sea with blue colour and it was touching the blue sky at the south. The name of the place is so called Neelachal as if an ornamented part of the Saree of Srimati Radharani. The waves one after another on the blue sea were coming and after touching the shore the beach they break.

During the discussion Sri Chaitanyadeva was also citing Harinaam in his lips but his fingers of the right hand was digging in the soft sands like the children dig sands for fun only. All were spectators of Sri Chaitanyadeva's fun play. Only Sri Gadadhara Pundit reacted and tried to advise Sri Chaitanyadeva - "Lord, what you are doing in the sands?"

Sri Chaitanyadeva slightly smiled to him but continued his fun play. All of a sudden keeping hand inside the sands Sri Chaitanyadeva called Sri Gadadhara Pundit and told - "Gadadhara my friend, see here I have found something under the sands. If I get anything here I like to give you as gift whatever it would be. Do you like to receive it?"

Sri Gadadhara Pundit replied humbly as usual manner - Lord, whatever you give me must I should receive."

Sri Chaitanyadeva lifting the hand said to him and other associates - "See, I can touch the top of my Prannatha I think. See here in the ditch."

Sri Chaitanyadeva called everybody and all with Sri Gadadhara Pundit bending their heads looked at the hole and became confident that there was a deity. Then all the associates started to dig the sands and ultimately a full sized deity of Lord Gopinath was found.

Sri Chaitanyadeva was highly pleased to find the deity and sang and danced with joy on the sea beach. All other people and his associates participated in the Sankirtan. The whole of the environment was filled with celestial of Sankirtan.

Then Sri Chaitanyadeva advised them to arrange to set the deity at the nearest 'Tota'. He also advised Sri Gadadhara Pundit to serve this beautiful deity of Gopinath every day.

Tour in South India

"Tomar Dui Hasta Baddha Naam Ganane..."

Thereafter in the 1432 Shaka (1510 AD) on the seventh day of Baisakh Sri Chaitanyadeva started his journey from Puri towards the south in order to distribute Harinaam to all at the places of pilgrims, villages and other localities. He wanted to go alone. But Sri Nityananda, Sri Gadadhara Pundit and all other well wishers raised objection that Sri Krishna Chaitanya Deva always remain in uttering the Lords name keeping his two hands up or would remain engaged in counting the 'Diksha Mantra' or Lord's name. At least for carrying his pot for water and inner and outer garments someone should accompany him. Sri Nityananda, Sri Gadadhara Pundit and other associates wanted to be company with him. He refused all of them by saying that they had lot of duties to have done.

Tomar Dui Hasta Baddha Naam Ganane,
Jalapatra Bahirbaas Bahibe Kemane.

(Ch.Ch. Madhya, Chap. IX)

At last one person Govinda whom Sri Chaitanyadeva used to call as Krishnadas was selected for doing the service.

Sri Krishnachaitanya in short Sri Chaitanyadeva travelled with Lord's name in his lips from Puri towards the eastern coast of the Bay of Bengal.

He said to others that he would go Kanyakumari and pretended that to find his elder brother Vishwarup who became an ascetic far before.

All his associates Sri Nityananda, Sri Gadadhara Pundit and others including Sri Sarbabhouma Bhattacharya, Sri Gopinath Acharya and some others accompanied him upto Alalnath. At Alalnath Sri Chaitanyadeva sang and danced in the Sankirtan at a temple. All and the local people were pleased with the unique Sankirtan led by him. But before arriving at Alalnath Sri Sarbabhouma Bhattacharya fell ill as a result of shock and he was advised to go back to Puri. Next day in the morning after taken bath Sri Chaitanyadeva started to run and did not look back even for a while.

Sri Chaitanyadeva was moving from the eastern side of the sea covering rivers, hills, forests, villages and the localities in the rains or scorching sunshine. He did not care any kind of obstacles on the way. He was moving sometime singing:-

Krishna Krishna Krishna Krishna Krishna Krishna Krishna He.
Krishna Krishna Krishna Krishna Krishna Krishna Krishna He.
Krishna Krishna Krishna Krishna Krishna Krishna Raksha Mum,
Krishna Krishna Krishna Krishna Krishna Krishna Pahi Mum,
Rama Raghaba Rama Raghaba Rama Raghaba Raksha Mum,
Krishna KeshavaKrishna KeshavaKrishna Keshava Pahi Mum.

(Ch.Ch. Madhya, Chap.IX)

Sri Chaitanyadeva reached nearer to Chilka Lake and there stayed at a Brahmin's house for the night. This Brahmin felt fortunate that Himself Lord Jagannathaswami with mecry has taken shelter at his house and from then the place was renamed as Jagannath Pur. The companion Krishnadas was following Sri Chaitanyadeva and while he failed to find Sri Chaitanyadeva running he just listened to the utterance of Harinaam or any of the songs towards Lord Sri Krishna.

Sri Chaitanyadeva in his south India travelling travelled many places starting from this **Jagannathpur** and thereafter at **Kurmasthan (Srikakulam), Sinhachalam, Vidyanagar, Mangalgiri, Pana Nrisinha, Srishailam, Abaloham, Siddha Bot, Skandha Khesetra, Sri Kaalhasti or Briddha Kashi, Thirupati - Thirumalai, Kanchipuram - Shiva Kanchi and Vishnu Kanchi, Mahabolipuram, Thiruvaur Vedaban, Pondicherry, Chidambaram, Gangaikonda Cholpuram, Malai Tirtha, Kumbhakonam, on the bank of the Cauveri Srirangam (Chaturmasya and Gopal Bhatta), Madurai, Puri Kamkosthi, Dakshina Mathura (twice), Durbeshan, Mahendra Hills and Rameswaram, Tamraparni**

at Pandyasthan, Kanyakumari, Vellimalai, Thiruvattur (Brhma Samhita), Kaladi village (Adiguru Shankaracharya), Guruvayur - Shringeri Mutt, Belur, Sahyadri Hills and Panchapsara-Yog Falls, Gokarna, Pottakodal, Surparak, Kolhapur, Pandharpur (Sri Rangapuri) and Dehu Village (Tukaram) at Pune, Mahabaleswar (Sri Krishnakarnamrita by Billwamongal), Tapti River, Narmada River and Omkareswar, Ujjain, Dhanutirtha, Panchvati, Brahmagiri, Trambakeswar, Dohad, Devghar, Shibaninagar, Malaya Hills, Chandipur, Raipur, Sapta Godavari and then to Vidyanagar on the bank of the Godavari and many other holy places of pilgrimage. Wherever he went he had immense respect for the deities and the place. He sang the Kirtan for love of Lord Sri Krishna and the deities of Sri Ramchandra, Shiva Mahadeva, Shaktidevi, Ganesha, Kartikeya and others. Almost the people and the devotees were pleased to find him with them: He was accepted by all.

At the time of beginning the tour on the bank of **the Godavari** where **Roy Ramananda** as an incharge of the area on behalf of **Raja Pratap Rudra king of Odisha** was ruling. The Philosophy of **'Sadhya Sadhan Tattwa'** was established in (10) ten days after discussion by Sri Chaitanyadeva and Roy Ramananda.

Sri Vrindabandas has referred at the 10th Chapter of Sri Chaitanya Bhagawata that Sri Chaitanyadeva toured upto Setubandha Rameswaram including devotion to Sri Ramchandra and giving salvation to the seven Palm Trees of Treta yuga.

Sri Krishnadas Kaviraj in the Chaitanyacharitamrita referred the South India travel in details.

Sri Chaitanyadeva at the end of Poush of 1433 Shaka after 1 year and 8 months travelling in the South India returned at the house of Roy Ramananda in Vidyanagar. He handed over the gifts two copies of the Books **'Brahma Samhita'** and **Sri Krishnakarnamrita by Billamangal** to Roy Ramananda. He arranged to make copies of the Books and He and Sri Chaitanyadeva also read them. After (7) seven days' stayal at Vidyanagar Sri Chaitanyadeva returned to Puri on the 3rd Magh of 1433 Shaka.

With the consultation with the King Pratap Rudra Sri Sarbabhoum Bhattacharya arranged the residence at the garden of Sri Kashi Mishra with his giving consent gladly. Then the place was famous in the name of 'Gambhira'.

All the people who were much anxious for his return were satisfied when he returned to Puri (Neelachal) and now they were eager to meet him and wanted to see him and have blessings from him too.

VI. Neelachal Leela 2

King Pratap Rudra wanted to Meet Sri Chaitanyadeva

The most honourable King Pratap Rudra of Odisha was engaged in political activities for a long time. He had heard the presence of Sri Chaitanyadeva in Puri and so, he had much eagerness to see and meet Sri Chaitanyadeva. Having returned to the palace of Puri-Neelachal His Highness King Pratap Rudra aspired to meet Sri Chaitanyadeva. Pundit Sarbabhoum Bhattacharya then informed the King that Sri Chaitanyadeva has gone to travel the South India.

Now, His Highness King Pratap Rudra again requested to try to arrange their meeting but at the first time he failed to do it. The reason behind it was that Sri Chaitanyadeva as a monk had no intention to be introduced with any King. But the King Pratap Rudra was an exception as he was the main sevak of Sri Sri Jagannath Mahaprabhu and possibly he had immense 'Bhakti' for Lord.

Moreover, from the top of the palace the King with Sarbabhoum Acharya got the opportunity of witnessing the divine songs and dances of Sri Chaitanyadeva with some associates and Kirtaniyas from Goud Bengal and also Odisha for love to Sri Sri Jagannath Mahaprabhu. With this his eagerness to meet Sri Sri Chaitanyadeva enhanced.

Earlier, one son of the King was allowed to meet Sri Chaitanyadeva and was blessed by him with an embracing with divinely satisfaction. But the thirst of meeting with Sri Chaitanyadeva of the King remained unfulfilled.

Lastly, the closed followers of Sri Chaitanyadeva advised the King the main Sevak of Sri Sri Jagannath Mahaprabhu to wait till the temple of Sri Sri Jagannath Mahaprabhu to be closed for the fortnight before the Rathayatra. Between the gap of 'Snan Yatra' and the Rathayatra the temple remains closed and at that time the regular routine of Sri Chaitanyadeva seeing straight the deities of Sri Sri Jagannath Mahaprabhu, Sri Sri Balarama and Sri Sri Suvadradevi from behind the Gdur Pillar remais paused. At that time Sri Chaitanyadeva had enough time to discuss the topics on Lord

Sri Krishna and to meet anyone if he allows. Sri Roy Ramananda, Sri Sarbabhoum Acharya and Kashi Mishra including Swarup Damodar planned to take the oppoutunity for the King and duly informed the King about this opportunity could be availed of.

One day during the period His Highness King Pratap Rudra leaving royal dresses behind and wearing ordinary dress entered the Garden where Sri Chaitanyadeva was discussing about the ensuing festival of Rathaytra of Sri Sri Jagannath Mahaprabhu. The king was singing from Sri Mad Bhagawata and fell down at the feet of Sri Chaitanyadeva who was listening to the nicely words of the Shloka that suited to him.

Jayati Tehadhikang Janmana Braja,
Shrayanta Indira Sha Shwadatra Hi;
Dayitang Drishyatang Dikshu,
Tabkastayi Dhritasabstang Bichinwate.

(Srimad Bhagawata 10/31/1)

Sri Chaitanyadeva was charmed to have listened the song that — O dear, with your appearing on the Brajabhumi it has gained its superiority to Baikuntha. Sri Lakshmidevi having adorned it herself preferred to remain in it. So, all inhabitants of Braja are happy. But Lord, the Gopis who are living for you only and are searching you after the separation. "O Lord, tell us where you are?"

Sri Chaitanyadeva lifted the King and embraced him cordially. The eyes of them were drenched with tears in love of Lord Sri Krishna.

To observe the signs of devotion in the King Sri Chaitanyadeva said - Always have the name of Sri Krishna, do Krishna naam Sankirtan and the Sudarshan would always protect you. I am here for you, Sarbabhoum and Roy Ramananda, the Trio only."

(Ch.Bh.Antya, Chap 5)

Sri Chaitanyadeva thus in Vaishnavism made an example of bridging people of high altitude and the people below the poverty line. His Highness King Pratap Rudra day after day was becoming more attracted to Vaishnavism and perhaps as per the advice of Sri Chaitanyadeva later was initiated from Sri Gadadhara Pundit.

Rajanang Srijutang Rudrang Pratapadyang Subishrytam,
Bande Gadadharo Yata Gouro Yena Susebitah.

(Gadadhara Shakha Nirnoy Grantha
by Kavi Karnapur)

Swarup Damodar Joined Sri Chaitanyadeva

Originally Sri Swarup Damodar in Nabadwip Leela was as Purushottam and active member of Harinaam Mahayagna. The sudden decision of taking Sannyas by beloved Sri Gouranga Mahaprabhu without informing him easily hurt him and made him offended. He could not bear the separation of his most beloved Sri Gouranga and so he left Nabadwip and went to Varanasi to be a Sannyasi. He was initiated by Chaitanyanda Acharya in Varanasi. He was named as Damodar but he remained in own style and was known as Swaroop Damodar. For his vast knowledge in scriptures he was given the charge of coaching the Upanishad to the other disciple of Acharya Chaitanyandas. However, his heart always ached for Sri Gouranga Mahaprabhu. He was fully acquired with the thoughts of Sri Gouranga and the Harinaam Sankirtan at Sri Sribaas 'Angan'. He passed almost two years in Varanasi. On being informed of Sri Chaitanyadev's return to Neelachal after the South India tour he opted to his preceptor to be with Sri Chaitanyadeva at Puri. The preceptor gladly allowed him to be with Sri Chaitanyadeva. He with a devotee of Sri Chaitanyadeva named Kamalakanta arrived at Neelachal.

In the Neelachal Leela Sri Swaroop Damodar was also considered the next to Sri Krishna Chaitanya Mahaprabhu. For his skill in scriptures and expertness in singing he was compared with Devaguru Brihaspati and Gandharva respectively. He engaged himself in controlling everything of Sri Chaitanyadeva. No one there dared to ask any question of his deeds for Sri Chaitanyadeva. He was the final on Sri Chaitanyadeva.

He used to protect Sri Chaitanyadeva from "falling off and on". He once cautioned Sri Chaitanyadeva while in engrossment in love to Sri Krishna was to run to a public female singer having listened to her devotional singing.

He also cautioned Sri Chaitanyadeva to meet a young affectionate boy who would come to him with his beautiful widow mother of young age.

He used to sing in the Kirtan by the side of Sri Chaitanyadeva. He shouldered many responsibilities till his death. He also taught Sri Raghunathdas as a teacher and guide as preferred and advised by Sri Chaitanyadeva.

Paramananda Puri's Well

From the South Sri Paramananda Puri went to Nabadwip and hearing Sri Chaitanyadeva's return from the South arrived at Neelachal and Sri Chaitanyadeva arranged his shelter in Puri.

Sri Paramananda Puri was one of the disciples of Sripad Madhabendra Puri. During the South India travel he met Sri Paramananda Puri and advised him not to travel here and there in his older days but to stay at a place for his sadhana. Only to be nearer to Sri Chaitanyadeva he agreed to settle in Puri.

Sri Chaitanyadeva once purified the Well at Sri Paramananda Puri's Shelter. Once the water of the well became somehow spoiled and the water could not be usuable as it was carrying filthy smelling. Sri Chaitanyadeva with some of his associates including Sri Gadadhara Pundit and others came and started the Sankirtan for hours. He by raising the two hands upward in love of Sri Jagannathaswami prayed the Ganga should come into the well.

On the next day again Sri Chaitanyadeva visited with all the well and found the water was magically changed as drinkable.

Sri Chaitanyadeva said to all and Sri Paramananda Puri - "Lord Jagannathaswami has listened to the prayer and brought the Ganga into the well. Let us start the Sankirtan again in love for Lord Sri Krishna Jagannathaswami". All of the associates became so pleased that everybody took water for drinking and began to sing and dance with Sri Chaitanyadeva.

Desire to Travel Vrindaban via Goud Banga

In the 4th Rathayatra of the 1437 Shaka the Goudiya Vaishnavas did not remain with Sri Chaitanyadeva after the Rathayatra as he much before the Rathayatra of the 1437 Shaka informed all the devotees of Goud that he planned to go to Vrindaban via Goud Bengal.

Janani Janhabi Ei Dui Dayamoy.
Goud Desh Diya Jabo Ta Sobha Dekhiya.

(Ch.Ch. Madhya, Chap XVI)

Sri Chaitanyadeva had not visited Sachimaa for long time. Although he was an ascetic he should not forget the mother. He felt the attraction of mother.

It may be mentioned that Adiguru Shankaracharya also did not forget his mother. Once during his travel throughout whole of India suddenly he felt the taste of mother's milk and leaving everything behind ran to mother while she was in death bed. She wanted to listen to the 'Stabas' written by him towards Lord. Adiguru Shankaracharya did the same for the happiness of his mother.

Feeling the silent call of mother and also the river Ganga Sri Chaitanyadeva decided to travel via Goud Bengal to Mathura-Vrindaban what he desired after taking Sannyas from Sri Keshab Bharati.

It was primarily decided that Sri Roy Ramananda, Sri Paramananda Puri, Sri Jagadananda, Sri Govinda, Sri Swaroop Damodar, Sri Gadadhara Pundit and some other devotees would be his company towards Mathura-Vrindaban.

According to Sri Chaitanya Charitamrita, Sri Paramananda Puri, Sri Swaroop Damodar, Sri Jagadananda, Sri Govinda, Sri Mukunda, Sri Haridas Thakura, Sri Pundit Bakreswar, Sri Gopinath Acharya. Sri Damodar Pundit, Sri Ramai, Sri Nandai, Sri Kashiswar and many others including Sri Gadadhara Pundit initially accompanied Sri Chaitanyadeva.

On the day of Vijaya Dashami Sri Chaitanyadeva having received Prasad, the threads to bind on the wrist and sandal wood paste what were given to Lord began his travel from Neelachal towards Goud Bengal. He reached **Bhawanipur** and Roy Ramamnanda also came here on a palanquin. Sri Baninath sent Prasad.

In the morning Sri Chaitanyadeva with all the people reached **Bhubaneswar.** Then he visited Sri Gopal at **Cuttack.** There Sri Swapneswar invited them all including Roy Ramananda. He took shelter at the garden under a 'Bakul' tree and Raja Pratap Rudra knew that Sri Chaitanyadeva has reached nearer to his capital. He then and there rushed to Sri Chaitanyadeva and was received cordially by embracing him. Roy Ramananda arranged a seat in front of Sri Chaitanyadeva. He prayed for the king's good in every respect to Lord Jagannathadeva. The people present there named Sri Chaitanyadeva as 'Pratap Rudra Santrata' . It meaned the Sri Chaitanyadeva was the savior of the Raja. The followers of the King also praised Sri Chaitanyadeva.

Then Raja Pratap Rudra arranged to send messages to all business men and monied people in his area to arrange shelters and sufficient food and also guard to Sri Chaitanyadeva and his company at the villages en route. Two Mahapatras Harichandan and Mardaraj were chosen to perform all the duties there. Raja also ordered to erect a pillar near the 'Ghat' of the river where Sri Chaitanyadeva would bathe. That 'Ghat' should be considered as a **'Mahatirtha'** and afterwards he would bathe regularly. He also ordered to erect new residence at **'Chaturdwar'** the village Chouda.

He also arranged the procession of the women in the cabinets on the decorated elephants. There the women after bathing in the river and receiving proper respect from all people had the privilege of darshan with full of open eyes the unprecedented divine look Sri Chaitanyadeva. All of them were overwhelmed for this scope of seeing Sri Chaitanyadeva crying and shedding tears from the eyes for Lord Sri Krishna. They at the same time also were fallen in love for Lord Sri Krishna.

At the moonlit night by a big boat Sri Chaitanyadeva crossed the river and reached 'Chaturdwar' the village Chouda. After taking rest there at night he bathed in the morning. And within a short time Prasad of Lord Jagannathadeva were carried to him by the 'Padichhas' as arranged by the King. This arrangement continued till Sri Chaitanyadeva remained in the area of the Raja. Sri Roy Ramananda, two Mahapatras Harichandan and Mardaraj these three were always ready to serve Sri Chaitanyadeva with his company.

Sri Chaitanyadeva then seeing Sri Gadadhara Pundit in the team of travelling remembered Lord Gopinath for whose service he was given the charge. So he planned to leave behind Sri Gadadhara Pundit for the uninterrupted regular service of Gopinathaji at Tota as taking 'Kshetra Sannyas'.

Gadadhara Pundit Yabe Sangete Chalila,
Kshetra Sannyas Na Chhadiyho Prabhu Nishedhila.
(Ch.Ch. Madhya, Chap XVI)

However, Sri Gadadhara Pundit did not want to leave the company of Sri Chaitanyadeva. Earlier at the time of his South India Tour almost two years he did not get the scope of the company of Sri Chaitanyadeva. Again, he was afraid that how many days would take in the Mathura-Vrindaban Tour is not ascertainable. He would not pass the long absence of Sri Chaitanyadeva. So, Sri Gadadhara Pundit replied that wherever Sri Chaitanyadeva remains, that place would be Neelachal or Mathura-Vrindaban or even Tota where Lord Gopinath remains. To have darshan of his feet is the more pious than anything in the Universe. Sri Chaitanyadeva tried to make him understand but Sri Gadadhara Pundit remained rigid.

Sri Chaitanyadeva then said to him - "Do not behave childish. If you leave service to Lord Gopinath and 'Kshetra Sannyas' the burden of your sins would be on me".

Sri Gadadhara Pundit at last started to go towards Goud Bengal by another route in order to see Sachimaa alone. Sri Chaitanyadeva then advised him to meet him and not to try to go by another route. He caught the hands of Sri Gadadhara Pundit and requested not to go.

Tanhar Charitre Prabhura Antare Santosh,
Tanhar Hathe Dhari Kahe Kori Pranay Rosh.

... ...

More Sukh Chaha Yadi Neelachale Chalo
Aamar Shapath Yadi Aar Kichhu Bolo.

(Ch.Ch, Madhya, Chap XVI)

Afterwards Sri Chaitanyadeva boarded in the boat and Sri Gadadhara Pundit fell down and fainted. Sri Chaitanyadeva advised Sarbabhouma Bhattacharya to take him to Neelachal. Sri Sarbabhoums did so and both of them returned Neelachal.

Sri Chaitanyadeva reached **Jajpur** and relieved the two Mahapatras Harichandan and Mardaraj. Sri Roy Ramananda remained with Sri Chaitanyadeva and they usually passed their time in discussion on Lord Sri Krishna and his eternal Love.

At each and every village the people of Raja Pratap Rudra engaged themselves as advised in performing the services of giving shelter in new built houses and supplying food to Sri Chaitanyadeva and his company.

At **Remuna,** Sri Chaitanyadeva now advised Sri Roy Ramananda to go back to Neelachal again. It was a shock to him also and he fell on the ground and became unconscious. Sri Chaitanyadeva took him up in his lap and cried for some time.

Thereafter, Sri Chaitanyadeva reached at the then border of Odisha and the people of the King two or three days remained to serve Sri Chaitanyadeva. Beyond the border there the heavily drunk Yaban Ruler a terror upto Pichhalda remains. In his fear no one could dare to cross the rivers.

During the stay of Sri Chaitanyadeva at Cuttack a spy of the ruler in disguise witnessed the glory of Sri Chaitanyadeva and informed to his master that the ascetic from Puri with many real devotees seems to be not harmful as he always remains in Harinaam Sankirtan. Thousands of the people meet him everyday. To see him he appears to be God. On hearing this from the spy the Yawan Ruler became a changed one and sent a reliable servant to Sri Chaitanyadeva to do the needful. With humble that person wanted to know where Sri Chaitanyadeva wants to go and Mukunda answered that all with Sri Chaitanyadeva want to go to the river Ganga. The Mahapatra of King Pratap Rudra was surprised and pleased and with love he embraced the person sent by the Yawan Ruler.

In the morning Sri Chaitanyadeva with all his companions boarded on a new boat and that person with a team of armed guards full of ten boats started to sail by giving guards the boat of Sri Chaitanyadeva and thus all of the team could cross the **Mantreswar** river upto **Pichhalda** safely.

Mantreswar Dushtanad Paar Karailo,
Pichhalda Paryanta Sei Yawan Aailo.
(Ch.Ch. Madhya, Chap XVI)

Sri Chaitanyadeva thanked the Yawan Ruler and all the persons who really were on duty to bring them upto their limit of boundaries at Pichhalda.

With the new boat supplied by the Yawan Ruler Sri Chaitanyadeva arrived at the 'Ghat' of **Panihati.** Here Sri Chaitanyadeva presented the sailors 'Kripa-Shati' and thanked a lot for their expertness.

Se Noukaya Chadi Prabhu Aaila Panihati,
Nabikere Prailo Nija Kripa-Shati.
(Ch.Ch. Madhya, Chap XVI)

All the people at Panihati and its adjacent areas assembled to have a darshan of Sri Chaitanyadeva. The crowd was so big that some of the people found space to stand in water. Sri Raghav Pundit hurriedly came forward and took Sri Chaitanyadeva at his house. Sri Chaitanyadeva remained at Panihati for a day and thereafter at Kumarhatta (Halisahar) where Sri Sribaas Pundit was residing since his Sannyas taking.

Thereafter, he had been at the house of Shibananda Sen at Kanchrapara. Later at Vidyanagar the earlier house of Sri Sarbabhoum Basudeva where Sri Vidyabachaspati another brother of Sri Sarbabhoum Basudeva was residing. They were the sons of Maheswar Visharad.

Sri Chaitanyadeva wanted to pass some days by bathing in the holy river Ganga and taking Harinaam alone being alienated from others for some rest. But thousands of people from different places started to come.

All at the front of the house of Vidyabachaspati the people in thousands assembled and shouted to see their loving Sri Chaitanya Mahaprabhu. All of them began Harinaam Sankirtan for the whole day for reaction of Mahaprabhu. Ultimately he came out of his stay and lifting his hands up sang Harinaam and thousands of people with their eagerness had the 'Darshan' with their satisfaction of earthly eyes. But they did not like to move after 'Darshan' and they remained at the front of the house. Day after day their numbers were increasing. The crowd so accumulated that it became beyond control. The roads and the jungles and bushes were full of the spectators including lame, blind, other physically handicapped persons and even lepers were also in the crowd. Sri Chaitanya Mahaprabhu felt the necessity of loneliness but it was not possible for the increasing crowd.

Srimukh Dekhiya Keha Ghare Nahi Jay.

(Ch.Bh.Antya, Chap 3)

In order to avoid the crowd one day before the dawn Sri Chaitanya Mahaprabhu with some of the company went to Kulianagar and reached the house of Sri Madhabdas Chattopadhaya. The fact was not informed to Sri Vidyabachaspati also.

On the other hand, the accumulated and the increasing crowd even after their Harinaam Sankirtan Sri Chaitanya Mahaprabhu did not come outside as he was not there. At first it was understood that Sri Vidyabachaspati he had hidden Sri Chaitanya Mahaprabhu from common people and then people began to blame that Sri Vidyabachaspati to get the blessings alone he has hidden him and so began to curse him.

Within a short period knowing the fact with the aggrieved people Sri Vidyabachaspati also went to **Kulianagar** and found Sri Chaitanya Mahaprabhu there. The place wherever Sri Chaitanya Mahaprabhu went became full of Sankirtan with playing different instruments and dances by all the devotees. The whole area became full of Sankirtan at different places.

Bhaja Bhaja Aare Bhai Chaitanyacharane,
Avidyabandhan Khande Jaharo Shravane,
Jaharo Shravane Sarbataap Bimochana,
Bhaja Bhaja Heno Nyasimonir Charana.
Ei Mate Chaturdike Dekhi Sankirtan,
Anande Bhasen Prabhu Loi Bhaktagana.

(Ch.Bh.Antya, Chap 3)

Here came **Sri Bakreswar Pundit** whose brilliant dances with Kirtan was preferred by Sri Chaitanya Mahaprabhu. He believed "Bakreswar-Hridaye-Krishna Nija Ghar". **Sri Devananda Pundit** who was learned but without devotion to Lord Sri Krishna used to coach and narrate Srimad Bhagawata attended the Kirtan with brilliant dances of Bakreswar. Sri Chaitanya Mahaprabhu advised him better he should have 'Bhakti' with his reading and coaching Srimad Bhagawata.

Here Sri Chaitanya Mahaprabhu condoned and forgave the sin earlier done by **Gopal Chapal.**

Also here as a courtesy visit **Tantrik Krishnananda Agambagish** who introduced the visible image of Maa Kali came as previously known to each other.

Sri Chaitanya Mahaprabhu then came to **Ramkeli** on the bank of the Ganga near Goud the capital of **Sultan Hussein Shah.** He remained some days with peace as he could bathe in the Ganga without any disturbances. But the news spread like wind that Sri Chaitanya Mahaprabhu was there and thousands of people gathered at the spot in order to have a darshan and also to participate in the Sankirtan.

There a Kotwal of Hussein Shah noticed him and accordingly informed Hussein Shah. Having learned the fact and the appearances of Sri Chaitanya Mahaprabhu he ordered all of his court not to disturb the monk and to allow him as many days he wants to live on the bank of the Ganga.

There came in disguise Amar and Santosh two brothers. One was appointed as the Prime Minister and the other was the Chief Secretary in the court of Sultan Hussein Shah. They were named as Sagir Mullick and Dabir Khas respectively. They bowed their heads at the feet of Sri Chaitanya Mahaprabhu. He accepted and named them as **Sanatan** and **Roop** respectively with unlimited pleasure.

They requested him not to stay more days at Ramkeli as Sultan might not take time to change his mood. Moreover, they also requested Mahaprabhu to please drop the intention to travel on foot to Mathura-Vrindaban for the time being as the routes fall under lawlessness areas. The political situations among the different Rulers or Kings were stern. So, almost disorderly situations might cause harm to the passers by in the time consuming long paths from Gaud to Mathura-Vrindaban. Sri Chaitanya Mahaprabhu then kept the programme in abeyance and declared to his men.

Sri Chaitanya Mahaprabhu then began to return to Neelachal by giving up the plan of travelling to Mathura-Vrindaban. On way he went to **Kanaier Natshala** and therafter reached **Shantipur** at the house of **Sri Adwaita Acharya.**

At Shantipur he met Sri Achyutananda son of Sri Adwaita Acharya. He was initiated from Sri Gadadhara Pundit. According to Haribhakti Vilas initiation by father is not the best so, with advice of Mahaprabhu or Sri Adwait Acharya himself the initiation of Sri Achyutananda from Sri Gadadhara Pundit was finalised. Sri Achyutananda was a loveable and affectionate young Vaishnava by Sri Chaitanyadeva, Sri Nityanandaprabhu, his preceptor Sri Gadadhara Pundit and other Vaishnavas.

Sri Adwaita Acharya having seen Sri Chaitanyadeva at his residence was very much pleased and he considered the sudden days of festivity have come to his residence. He sent a palanquin to Nabadwip to bring Sachimaa so that she could meet her son after a few years. On her arrival there Sri Chaitanyadeva fell at the feet of mother and cried much by saying mother's debt cannot be repaid by any means any time in lives after lives. She took him up and with the permission entered the kitchen and in order to prepare various items preferred by Sri Gouranga for offering to Lord Sri Krishna. Later having offered to Lord by Sri Adwaita Acharya Sachimaa distributed Prasad to Sri Chaitanyadeva, Sri Adwaita Acharya and the devotees who were present there.

There at the second time Raghunath Das from Tribeni was present with his escorts provided by his father and elder uncle.

Then Sri Chaitanyadeva reached the house of Sri Sribaas Pundit. At the time of going towards Ramkeli he was in a hurry so he could not stay much time at **Kumarhatta.** Now he was returning to Neelachal and he wanted to stay some days with his beloved senior Sri Sribaas Pundit and both recollected the days of Harinaam Sankirtan.

Here came Sri Shibananda Sen, Sri Basudeva Dutta, Sri Purandar Acharya and other followers. All met in the Sankirtan by which the house became full of spirits. However, Mahaprabhu somehow could understand that Sri Sribaas's pecuniary conditions were not satisfactory enough. He could easily feel that Sribaas had no efforts to earn money by visiting the houses of his disciples. Rather he preferred to remain at home for worshipping Lord Sri Krishna and Sri Chaitanya Mahaprabhu. He was a real Sadhaka but for maintaining own family he needed some financial assistance. Mahaprabhu then called his brothers and advised them to provide necessary help so that he could continue his services to God without any headache of earnings.

Sri Chaitanya Mahaprabhu reached **Khardah** and advised Sri Nityanandaprabhu to find a place to inhabit as the place and the people were his likings. He also advised him to start family life after marriage. He also reminded Sri Nityanandaprabhu not to be in Puri every year.

Afterwards, Sri Chaitanya Mahaprabhu arrived at the house of Sri Raghav Pundit at **Panihati** on the bank of the Ganga. There many people from different places like Sodepur, Natagarh, Sukhchar, Agarpara,

Belghoria, Naodapara, Ariadah, Khardah, also Konnagar, Hooghly, etc thronged there.

Among them were Sri Makardhwaz Kar from Sukhchar, Sri Gadadhar Das (known as Das Gadadhar) from Ariadah, Sri Purandar Pundit, Sri Parameswardas from Hooghly, Sri Raghunath Vaidya and many others followers of Sri Chaitanya Mahaprabhu. He advised Sri Makardhwaz Kar to have care so that Sri Raghav Pundit could not spend money extravagantly all whatever he would earn the money at a time. He was required to be more serious for the services of the guests and devotees in future. In both the cases at Panihati and at Kumarhatta at the house of Sri Sribaas Sri Chaitanya Mahaprabhu was like a practical personality for his followers.

Afterwards Sri Chaitanya Mahaprabhu came to Baranagar on the bank of the Ganga. Here resides Sri Raghunath Upadhyaya who was initiated from Sri Gadadhara Pundit earlier at Nabadwip as advised by Mahaprabhu then. Now he became overwhelmed to see Sri Chaitanya Mahaprabhu at his hut under a tree Margosa. Almost the whole night he read the Srimad Bhagawata and Mahaprabhu listened to the reading and he danced in love for Lord Sri Krishna. Ultimately, Mahaprabhu declared him as 'Bhagawatacharya'. Since then the place was named as Pathbari.

Sri Chaitanyadeva returned to Neelachal

Thereafter Sri Chaitanyadeva returned to Neelachal in the summer of 1438 Shaka much before scheduled time. To find him his lifetime beloved friend Sri Gadadhara Pundit became surprised and was pleased. However, knowing the postponement of Mathura-Vrindaban tour he was sad. Laughingly Sri Chaitanyadeva said - I left Gadahara here so I was feeling guilty. I too got pain".

Gadadhare Chhari Gelam Inho Dukhah Paailo,
Sei Hetu Vrindaban Jaaite Naarilo.

(Ch.Ch. Madhya, Chap XVI)

Sri Gadadhara Pundit knowing it was nothing but a joke said to Sri Chaitanyadeva - I know for teaching to others you ought to go here and there and I should not prohibit you to go. It would be better to travel after the rainy season".

All the associates nodded their heads in support of Gadadhara's suggestion. However, he invited Sri Chaitanyadeva and all the accompanying devotees to take Prasad of Sri Sri Gopinathji on the day and it was accepted.

Raghav's Jhali

Every year before Rathayatra from Panihati situated on the bank of the Ganga in the district of North 24 Parganas of West Bengal (opposite of Konnagar in the district of Hooghly). Sri Raghav Pundit of Panihati along with Sri Makardhwaz Kar of nearest village Sukhchar with two or three labourers brings dried food for consumtion by Sri Chaitanyadeva at the rest of the year in Neelachal. All the foods are prepared by sister Srimati Dayamanti Devi throughout the whole year.

With proper care and devotion Dayamanti Devi used to prepare and dry up the foodstuff in the Sunrays various types of different laddus, mango-pieces with liquid mustard oil paste, ginger with mustard oil paste, ginger with lemon juice, mango-buds, mango pieces, oiled mango, mangopaste (Aamsattwa), old powder of bitter leaves, laddu of coriander and aniseed powder mixed with sugar, jujube, dried jujube, jujube powder, coconut laddu, coconut pieces, water of the Ganga, condensed milk and camphor, veg chida, mudki, fried chida, laddu of rice fried in ghee, black pepper powder, big laddus of different rice made chida and khai, mango pickles and sauces of different fruits etc. These were taken in bags and containers what were carried by at least three helpers.

Gundicha Margan

Sri Chaitanyadeva reached Neelachal at the end of the year 1431 Shaka and, thereafter, at the beginning of 1432 Shaka he went to travel South India and travelled almost two years. From the year 1434 Shaka he participated in the Rathayatra of Lord Jagannatha Mahaprabhu. During the Rathayatra the deities of Sri Sri Jagannatha, Sri Sri Balarama and Sri Sri Subhadradevi along with divine weapon Sudarshan are received at the Gundicha Temple having halt at Aunt's house (Masir Bari) at Bolgandi. There millions of devotees from all over India and also from foreign countries assemble and prefer to draw the ropes of the chariots.

Sri Chaitanyadeva had the clear concept of keeping clean the places and the environment for good health. He had the practice of cleanliness even at Nabadwip. In many of the temples there and at place of Harinaam Sankirtan Movement he used to advance with team for the work of cleaning.

In Neelachal Sri Chaitanyadeva decided to clean the floors and other places including the throne at the Gundicha Temple where millions of devotees from differen places of the country usually assemble to have darshan of Lord Jagannatha and his accompanying deities. So, being informed the King ordered his men to supply one hundred brooms and pots for Sri Chaitanyadeva and his accompanying devotees for the purpose. Sri Chaitanyadeva also himself did the manual work with proper care and strict supervision . He also used his saffron wrapper to accumulate the dust of the temple and to throw outside the temple.

This whole day job has since then become conventional for every year before the Rathayatra.

Rathayatragre Sri Chaitanyadeva

The Rathayatra of Sri Sri Jagannath-Balarama-Subhadra and Sudershan drawn by three chariots from main Temple to Gundicha Temple is commences on the day of dwitiya (2nd day of bright fortnight) and continues till the ekadashi (11th day of bright fortnight) all as per Madia Panji (Panjika) of the Temple.

In the book Sri Sri Chaitanyacharitamrita we find only an elaborate discussion of the Rathayatra for one occasion. It is true that the author Sri Krishnadas Kaviraj while began to write the divine Life Sketch of Sri Krishnachaitanya as advised by Sri Nityanandaprabhu he received materials from different sources. The sources were Sri Chaitanya Bhagwata by Sri Vrindabandas, some writings of Swarup Damodar, the day-to-day experiences for long sixteen years' stay in Puri and what noted the information acquired by Sri Raghunath Das. There may be some writings of Sri Chaitanyadeva including the Shiksha Shlokastaka and Sri Sri Jaganathastaka what Sri Raghunath Das carried from Puri to Vridaban. The sources of Kaviraja's materials were also from writings of Kavi Karnapur there and he also mentioned references from old scriptures and also from other composers like Murari Gupta, Lochandas, Sri Roop and Sri Sanatan and other devotees who worked on the divine life of Sri Chaitanyadeva.

In the book Sri Sri Chaitanyacharitamrita we find the greatest Rathayatra of Sri Sri Jagannath-Balarama-Subhadra and divine weapon Sudershan drawn by three chariots from main Temple to Gundicha Temple thousands of devotees from Goud Bengal and other parts used to come on foot or bullock-curts or palanquins.

The author has described that very early in the morning having bathed Sri Chaitanyadeva started for seeing the 'Pandu Vijay' (the riding of the deities on the Chariots) alongwith own associates like Sri Adwita, Sri

Nityananda and other devotees. His Highness King Raja Pratap Rudra arranged for darshan of them. There were strong and stout like elephants the 'Pandas' having tied their waist with 'Patta Dari' did the job placing on cotton made pillows the Deities one after another. Sri Chaitanyadeva shouted with all 'Manima' that indicates in Odishi Language the greatest one. Sri Chaitanyadeva was surprised to note that the His Highness King himself cleansed the path with broom made of Gold and washed there with sandal wood water.

There were hundreds of colourful flags, chamor (fly-whisks) and canopies in order to greet Sri Sri Jagannath-Balarama-Subhadra and divine weapon Sudershan. Mahaprabhu Sri Sri Jagannath after a fortnight's rest and divine Lila lastly came out to please the devotees.

In an occasion of the Rathayatra after the Pandu Vijay and cleaning the path by Golden broom and sandalwood mixed water the Rathas as the custom were being drawn by the horses but they did not move. The King with his associates came forward and they decided to pull the Ratha by the eminent wrestlers but the Ratha did not move. Then the King ordered his men to bring the elephants from their stables. The elephants tried to pull the Ratha but the Rathas remained stagnant.

Then Sri Chaitanyadeva with the devotees and associates could not remain as spectators. He gave the rope of the Rathas to his men from Goud Bengal to pull and he himself pushed with forehead the Ratha of Lord Jagannathaswami from the back and the Ratha began to move smoothly.

Aapani Rathera Pachhe Thele Matha Diya,
Harh Harh Kari Ratha Chalila Dhaiya.
Vaktagan Kachhite Hath Diya Matra Dhay,
Aapane Chalaye Rath Tanite Na Paay.

All the people shouted 'Jay Jagannath' 'Jay Jagannath' 'Jay Jagannath' 'Jay Jagannath' and within a short time the Ratha reached the gate of Gundicha Temple. Then 'Pandu Vijay' was done by the Sevakas and on the throne Sri Sri Jagannath-Balarama-Subhadra and Sudershan were set. Sri Chaitanyadeva began to sing and dance with all his associates. The King and all others having seen this glorius incident done by Sri Chaitanyadeva were surprised.

(Ch. Ch. By Krishnadas Kaviraj 2/14)

The Rathas were being drawn by the people from different places and the devotees of Goud Bengal with pleasure and Sankirtan, dances on the path towards Gundicha Temple. Sometime the Rathas get speed, sometime they run slowly and sometime they take a break for a halt.

Sri Chaitanyadeva garlanded and painted with sandal wood paste all the devotees like Sri Paramanda Puri, Sri Keshab Bharati, Sri Brhmananda, Sri Adwitacharya, Sri Nityananda, probably Sri Gadadhara Pundit, Sri Swarup, Sri Sribaas, the singers of the four teams and two madarngiks (who play with Mridanga) in each team. Then Sri Chaitanyadeva advised Sri Nityananda, Sri Adwaitacharya, Sri Haridas Thakur, Sri Bakreswar to dance in the procession. He selected in the first team as the main Sri Swarup with five persons for 'Pali' (Dohar) songs. He also engaged Sri Damodar, Sri Raghav Pundit, Sri Narayan Dutta, Sri Govinda, Sri Govindananda and Sri Adwaitacharya for dance in the team.

In another team he selected Sri Sribaas as the leader where Sri Gangadas, Sri Haridas, Sri Sriman, Sri Shubhananda, Sri Ram Pundit were present. He selected for dancing Sri Nityananda and for singing Sri Basudeva, Sri Gopinath and Sri Murari.

In the third team Sri Chaitanyadeva selected Sri Mukunda as the chief singer where Sri Srikanta and Sri Ballav Sen were included. Sri Haridas Thakur was there for dancing.

In the fourth team Sri Chaitanyadeva selected Sri Govinda Ghosh as the chief singer wherein Sri Haridas, Sri Vishnudas, Sri Raghav also sing and there remain two brothers like Madhav and Basudeva. Therein Sri Bakreswar Pundit was selected to perform dance programmes.

The four teams were not enough to accept all other singers so Sri Chaitanyadeva planned to accommodate all in more three groups of them.

A group of singers were from Kulin Gram wherein Sri Ramananda Satyaraj dances.

Another team from Shantipur of Acharya Sri Adwaita was present in the Rathayatra. There were Sri Achyutananda, one son of Sri Adwaita and other singers and players.

The seventh team of Sri Khanda comprising Sri Narahari Sarkar for dances with Sri Raghunandan there.

At the front of the Rathayatra there were the four teams, on the sides were two teams and at the back was one team to sing. All the seven teams with fourteen big drums started to perform the Kirtan with the sound all over Puri and the sea, the sky everywhere.

At the seven teams Sri Chaitanyadeva in a loud voice called 'Hari' 'Hari' and 'Joy Jay Jagannath'. It was a surprise that all the people of the teams noticed that Sri Chaitanyadeva was in their teams. Sri Sri Jagannath Mahaprabu as if Himself having a halt of the Ratha enjoyed the singing and dancing with sounds of defferent instruments many a time.

The King Pratap Rudra was highly astonished to see Sri Chaitanyadeva at the same time was in the seven teams at reasonable distances singing and dancing with loudly playing the available musical instruments. He said to Sri Kashi Mishra and Sri Sarbabhoum Acharya. They replied to the King that he was a fortunate personality. The mystery is only known to Lord Brahma. The King for his service to Sri Sri Jagannathaswami made Sri Chaitanyadeva was pleased so much. Both of Sri Kashi Mishra and Sri Sarbabhoum Acharya were also surprised to note the pleasure of the King.

In the procession of the Rathayatra Sri Chaitanyadeva was seen in different appearances including Vrindaban Lila and Goud Lila.

The author of the book Sri Sri Chaitanyacharitamrita here reminds us the Shlokas recited by Sri Chaitanyadeva from the Srimad Bhagawata, Mukundamalaam Padaboli, the Vishnu Purana, the Mahabharata-Shanti Parba and others scriptures. One of them was:-

Namo Brahmanydevay Gobrahmanahitayh Cha,
Jagadhitaya Krishnaya Gobindaya Namo Namah.

(the Vishnu Purana 1/19/65,
the Mahabharata-Shanti Parba 47/94)

The meaning of the Shloka is that, "Who is worshippable by the people conversant with the Vedas, who is benefactor of Cows Brahmins and benefactor of the Universe and keeper of the cows I bow my head repeatedly to Him".

Let us re-continue from Sri Sri Chaitanyacharitamrita that all the devotees bowed their heads by folding their two hands. Sri Chaitanyadeva roaring sang and danced and all others also participated with him and sang and danced encircling him. There were stagnation, sweats, tears in joy, trembling and fading colour while he was dancing indomitably.

Once, Sri Chaitanyadeva fell on the ground. Then Sri Nityananda lifted him and Adwaita Acharya also roared in the name of God. Sri Haridas uttered Haribol Haribol repeatedly.

Afterwards, when the crowd was some thinner there were three circles keeping Sri Chaitanyadeva in the centure. In the first circle Sri Nityananda,

Sri Kashiswar, Sri Govinda and other devotees were present. In the second circle the devotees held the hands of each other.

Outside the two circles King Pratap Rudra placing his hand on Sri Harichandan and with other associates was enjoying the divine form of dances by Sri Chaitanyadeva. Seeing Sri Harichandan as an obstacle to peruse the singing and dancing Sri Sribaas made an awkward situation but the King himself mitigated by saying to Sri Harichandan - This was your fortune that you have been touched by the real devotee like Sri Sribaas, one of the closed associates of Sri Chaitanyadeva".

To witness the singing and dances by Sri Chaitanyadeva Sri Sri Jagannathaswami also seemed to be more cheerful. He with His elder brother and lovely sister stares at the programme with eyes open all the time by making a halt.

Sri Chaitanyadeva while singing and dancing for Lord some signs of pure eight 'Swatwik' in mood. There were some of acnes on his body with the emotion for God. His teeth were trembling violently. With the sweat it was bleeding speedily like syringes. He tried to spell Jagannathaswami but could not, instead the sound like "Jaja Gaga Jaja Gaga" nothing more audible came out. Like fountain tears were running. All the people around him were drenched with the sweat and tears what came out from him. Sometime Sri Chaitanyadeva fell on the ground with stiff limbs like made of wood. The devotees became speechless. Sometime water from his nose fell on his mouth and also there were foam at his mouth what Sri Shubhananda received and drank in love of Lord and Sri Chaitanyadeva. Thus with the singing and unresistable dancing he with emotion stopped and advised Swarup to continue singing and dancing.

Then Swarup Damodar began to sing:-

Seito Prananatha Pailoon
Zaha Lagi Madana Mohane Jhuri Geloon.

(Padam)

Sri Swarup Damodar was singing loudly. Then Sri Chaitanyadeva having looked at Sri Sri Jagannathaswami again began to dance slowly but nicely. Others by keeping eyes at Sri Sri Jagannathaswami participated in the singing and all followed Sri Chaitanyadeva. He was emerged in thought of Sri Sri Jagannathaswami. Where Sri Gouranga remains back the Rathas were stopped. When he advances the Rathas began to move following him slowly.

While dancing so nicely Sri Chaitanyadeva had to change his mood and sang:-

Jah Koumaraharah Sau Eba Hi Brasta Eba Chaitrakshpaste
Chonmllimalatisuravoyah Prourhah Kadambaneelah,
Sa Choibasmi Tathapi Tatra Suratabyaparleelabidhou
Rebarodhasi Betasitarutale Chatah Samutknthte.

Only Sri Swarup Damodar knew the meaning of this Shloka - A certain heroin was informing her confidante that he who had broken her virginity now is her husband. At the time of the first union that was a night of 'Chaitra' and now also the night of 'Chaitra' has come. Like that night the fragrance of blossomed 'Malati' also blowing the air slowly. See I am here. But I feel extremely distressed remembering the unison of us at the bank of the river Reba under a cane plant."

(In Kavy Puran 1/4, Sahitya Darpan 1110, Padaboli 386)

In emotion Sri Chaitanyadeva repeatedly sang the Shloka.

In the Bhagawata there remains this (Radhika) Bachan and that has been described. Sri Chaitanyadeva recited this Shloka and only Sri Swarup Damodar knew this and afterwards Sri Roop Goswami explained where Sri Swarup Damodar received it.

The author explained the song as once in Kurukshetra in the occasion of a rare Solar Eclips where all the Gopis assembled to see Sri Krishna with much pleasure and eagerness. Sri Chaitanyadeva with emotion sang towards Sri Sri Radhakrishna:-

"Abasheshe Sei Tumi Sei Aami Se Naba-Sangam .
Tathapi Aamar Mon Hare Vrindaban,
Vrindabane Udaya Karaha Aapon Charan.
Inha Lokarany Hathi-Ghora Rathadhwani,
Tanha Pishparany Bhringa-Pik-Nad shuni.
Inha Rajabesh Sob Kshatriya Gan,
Tanha Gopagan Sange Muralee-Badan.
Braje Tomar Sange Zei Sukh-Aaswadan
Sei Sukh Samudrer Inha Nahi Eka Kon.
Aama Laiya Punah Leela Kara Vrindabane,
Tabe Aamar Manobanchha Hoy Tau Purane..."

(Ch. Ch. By Krishnadas Kaviraj *2/13)*

All the divine Lilas of Lord Radhakrishna Sri Chaitanyadeva used to discuss with Sri Swarup Damodar day and night. In the dances and songs Sri Chaitanyadeva recited during the Rathayatra seeing Sri Sri Jagannathaswami.

With extreme emotion Sri Chaitanyadeva looks at the face of Lord Jagannathaswami whose ornaments were coruscating with the sunrays. In Sri Chaitanyadeva all the moods as Swattwik, Sanchari, Sthayee etc were observed. Sri Chaitanyadeva was so soft as flower and pure. Sri Chaitanyadeva also drenched the people with sweat and tears as the rain of love to all the devotees. All the people of Odisha, Goud Bengal and from other places including the associates of the King were surprised to witness the activities of Sri Chaitanyadeva in the Rathayatra.

All were inspired to sing, dance and to participate in the Rathayatra by serving for Lord Jagannathaswami. At Bolgandi what was called 'Masir Bari' hundreds of people offered 'Bhog' of different palatable dishes in earthen pots. There in a flower garden Sri Chaitanyadeva took rest with all singers and players.

Then at the gate of Gundicha Temple Sri Chaitanyadeva danced in indomitableness among all the seven teams and made the devotees to dance. Sri Sribaas, Sri Ramai, Sri Raghu, Sri Govinda, Sri Mukunda, Sri Haridas, Sri Govindananda, Sri Madhav, Sri Govinda (another) all these nine sang with Sri Swarup. These ten devotees sang encircling Sri Chaitanyadeva. The members of other teams also sang around them. All bowed their heads and sang with glorification of Lord Jagannathaswami.

The descriptions of being at the front of the Rathayatra have been stated in the Chaitanyastaka by Sri Roop Goswami.

Ratharurasyaradadhipadabi
Neelchalpateradavrapremormisfuritnatanollasabibash:.
Saharshang Gayadvih Paribritatanurboishnavjanoih
Sau Chaitanyah King Me Punarapi Drishorzasyti Padam.

- He who with highly pleasure danced and sang and overwhelmed becoming almost mad and paralised at the front of Sri Sri Jagannathaswami in the Ratahayatra that Sri Chaitanyadeva surrounded by singing Vaishnavas whether would come again in the path of our vision?

(Stabamala by Sri Roop Goswami 1st Staba 7th Shloka)
(All above from Sri Sri Chaitanyacharitamrita
by Sri Krishnadas Kaviraj, 2/13)

In the Sri Sri Chaitanyacharitamrita by Sri Krishnadas Kaviraj although elaborately described only one occasion of the Rathayatra of Lord Jagannathaswami but he also described some portions relating the Rathayatra in other chapters.

Till Sri Chaitanyadeva's presence the people from Goud Bengal would gather in every occasion of the Rathayatra since 1434 (1512 AD) Shakabda.

In 1434 Shakabda thousands of spectators from Goud Bengal would reach in the month of Ashada (June-July) Puri in order to witness the Rathayatra of Lord Jagannathaswami and their loveable Sri Gouranga - Sri Chaitanyadeva, after his return from the travelling in the South India. They, including Sri Nityananda, remained there for four months (Chaturmasya) till the 'Uththan Dwadashi' in the month of Kartick (October-November). Thereafter, Sri Chaitanyadeva advised Sri Nityanandaprabhu not to come in Neelachal in every occasion of the Rathayatra better he should take up the work of distribution of Harinaam. He knew the task was so big that only one person might not succeed to distribute Harinaam in the whole Bengal and also other places. So, he advised him to take along (1) Ramdas, (2) Gadadhardas (known as Das Gadadhar), (3) Raghunath Bejojha, (4) Krishnadas Pundit, (5) Parameswardas, (6) Puranadar Pundit and some others.

The associates who were called Gopal or Upa-Gopal also accompanied Sri Nityananda.

In 1435 Shaka (1513 AD) also thousands of spectators and their wives from Goud Bengal reached in the month of Ashada (June-July) Puri in order to witness the Rathayatra of Lord Jagannathaswami and their loveable Sri Gouranga - Sri Chaitanyadeva. The wives of the associates also took with them the spices and other materials for cooking for their own person Sri Namai-Sri Gouranga-Sri Chaitanyadeva.

In 1436 Shaka (1514 AD) people who reached Puri in order to witness the Rathayatra of Lord Jagannathaswami and their loveable Sri Gouranga. They did not remain four months as in other years and returned to Goud Bengal after the Rathayatra. Sri Nityananda brought one maund of nice rice and beautiful dress for Lord Gopinath being worshipped by Sri Gadadhara Pundit at Tota. Here the trio Sri Nityananda, Sri Gadadhara Pundit and Sri Gouranga - Sri Chaitanyadeva took Prasad. The Prasad was cooked by Sri Gadadhara Pundit himself for Lord Gopinatha. The Trio roamed in Neelachal for some days.

In 1437 Shaka (1515 AD) people did not visit Puri as Sri Chaitanyadeva had a plan to visit Mathura-Vrindaban. But he could not go further from

Ramkeli and other places and having met many people like Sri Sanatan, Sri Roop, Sri Nityananda, Sri Sribaas, Sri Adwaitacharya and others as he had to cancel the plan to visit Mathura-Vrindaban this time only.

In 1438 Shaka (1516 AD) many people and also a certain dog along with Sri Shibananda Sen went to Puri. The dog remained at the feet of Sri Chaitanyadeva. It gladly used to eat everything what Sri Chaitanyadeva ate even a coconut gladly. At this occasion Sri Swarup Damodar, Sri Nityananda, Sri Gadadhara Pundit, Sri Adwitacharya, Sri Haridas and all other associates were introduced with Sri Roop Goswami. Sri Chaitanyadeva asked for blessing from them for Sri Roop Goswami. Sri Roop Goswami here decided to write two separate dramas on Lord Sri Krishna 'Lalita Madhav' and 'Bidagdha Madhav' as advised in dream by the Queen Satyabhama on his way to Neelachal. Sri Chaitanyadeva was also happy to learn this. He told Sri Roop -

"Krishnake Bahir Nahi Brja Haite,
Braja Chhari Krishna Kavu Na Zaan Kahate."

(Ch. Ch. By Krishnadas Kaviraj 3/1)

In 1439 Shaka (1517 AD) the devotees and other spectators reached Puri in order to witness the Rathayatra of Lord Jagannathaswami and their loveable Sri Chaitanyadeva. Sri Adwita, Sri Gadadhara, Sri Swarup Damodar and Sri Nityananda were introduced with Sri Sanatan who from the way of Jharikhand arrived at Neelachal.

In 1440 Shaka (1518 AD) the devotees, huge number of the singers and players of musical instruments and many ordinary people were present in Neelachal.

Probably Sri Krishnadas Kaviraj has elaborately discussed this occasion where the seven groups of singers and players were present.

In 1441 Shaka (1519 AD) with the team of pilgrimages, as ususal arranged by Sri Shibananda Sen, Sri Nityananda also reached Puri to have a darshan of his life Sri Chaitanyadeva. On the way of coming to Neelachal he had some differences of opinions with Sri Shibananda Sen. All the Vaishnavas call it was nothing but 'Prem Kalaha'.

Goudiya Vaishnavas in Neelachal

After Sri Chaitanyadeva's return from the South in 1434 Shaka the Goudiya Vaishnavas all assembled in Neelachal to witness the Mega Ratha Yatra of Lord Jagannath in the month of Ashada and to pass the

'Chaturmasya' with their beloved Sri Chaitanyadeva. They with Sri Nityananda and all witnessed the Neelachal Leela of Sri Chaitanyadeva.

Sri Shibananda Sen one of the followers of Sri Chaitanyadeva was the organiser of the tour for the people of Gaud Bengal. He as a guide takes the pilgrims towards Neelachal and arranges the temporary residences there for their stayal.

In the month of Ashada on the 2nd day of Shukla Sri Sri Jagannathadeva with His elder brother Sri Sri Balarama and their affectionate sister Subhadra Devi and also divine Sudarshan are placed on the Ratha. While the King Pratap Rudra himself taking the broom made of gold cleaned the path of the Ratha Sri Chaitanyadeva was surprised to note the greatness of the King. Sri Chaitanyadeva also noted that despite the strong people began to pull the Ratha but no movement was found. The elephants were brought and having tied with the ropes they pulled the Ratha but it did not move. Sri Chaitanyadeva was puzzled for some time and thought that thousands of the spectators waiting for the Rathayatra could be deployed in the task of pulling the Ratha. He placed his suggestion and after some discusions among the priests of the temple and the King the change of customs as were the suggestion was accepted. Sri Chaitanyadeva called irrespective of caste and colour thousands of the spectators and the devotees from Gaud Bengal assembled there. All then began to pull the cord, strong and long, but the Ratha did not move. At last, Sri Chaitanyadeva himself from behind the Ratha pushed it with his forehead and all pulled the rope with enthusiasm uttering Harinaam loudly and the Ratha began to move.

Sri Chaitanyadeva sang Harinaam and danced in love to Sri Sri Jagannathadevaswami on the way of the Ratha. All the Kirtaniyas also participated in singing and dancing all along.

The Goudiya Vaishnavas after the Rathayatra and having met with their beloved Sri Chaitanyadeva for long four months in the month of Kartik and after the Uththan Dwadashi returned Bengal with ached hearts because they generally did not want to leave their beloved Sri Chaitanyadeva behind.

Sri Nityananda remained some days more for some discussion with Sri Chaitanyadeva.

He advised Sri Nityananda to go back to Gaud Banga and continue the Harinaam Love to God Sri Krishna to all there.

Nityanandang Samalingya Ditwa Tasya Kardwayam,
Praha Sau Gadgadang Yahi Gouddeshng Twamishwarah.

(in Sanskrit by Murari Gupta in the Kadcha)

Followers in Odisha

Like the followers in Bengal many of the people here in Odisha also became serious followers of Sri Krishnachaitanya or Sri Chaitanyadeva while he was in 'Gambhira'. It is a hard job to collect the names and their identities after more than 500 years. However, let us remember with due respect a few of them who were the serious followers like Sri Ramananda, Janardan, Krishnadas, Shikhi Mahiti, Pradyumna Mishra, Premananda, Damodar Pundit, Sri Shankar Pundit, Sri Bhagawan Acharya, Pradyumna Brahmachari, Jagannatha Maha Soar, Murari Mahiti, Chandaneswar, Sinheswar, Murari Bipra, Sri Tulsi Padichha, Sri Dalui or Dwarpal Ananta Pratihari, Sri Das Mahasoar, Krishnananda Odra, Shibananda Odra, Vishnudas, Praharaj Mahapatra, Pramananda Mahapatra, Bhabananda Roy (father of Roy Ramananda) with his five sons one of them was Baninatha for the service of Sri Chaitanyadeva, Kanai Khuntia, the two Mahapatras Harichandan and Mardaraj and many many others.

We have also known the name of Srimati Madhuri Mahiti who used to write poems also. She being a poet and follower of Sri Chaitanyadeva once expressed her pain of becoming a woman and wrote:-

Dakshine Netai Bosi Bame Gadadhara,
Mililen Gorachandera Yata Anuchara.
Ye Dekhayae Gorarupa Sei Preme Bhase,
Madhabi Bonchita Hoiya Nija Karmadoshe.

(Bangiya Sahitya Parishad Patrika, 1305 BS,
3rd Issue Stri Kavi Madhabi)

VII. Travel to Mathura-Vrindaban

Walking through the Forest of Jharikhand

Sri Chaitanyadeva ultimately was succeded to travel Mathura-Vrindaban. In the Season Autumn of 1438 Shaka after the Vijaya Dashami, very early in the morning without any public announcement with Sri Balabhadra Bhattacharya and one Brahmin helper Sri Chaitanyadeva set for Mathura-Vrindaban.

He avoiding regular way keeping Cuttack at the right side entered the forest areas of Jharikhand where various animals inhabitated freely. During the forest path Sri Chaitanyadeva had to face Tigers, Elephants, Deers and many other beasts with teeth and nails and also birds small or big. But Sri Chaitanyadeva needed not to stop for them and he continued Harinaam in his lips. No danger from them was occurred. He with his two companies reached the village of the Veels in the forest and was received by them for his Harinaam Singing.

Jhaarikhande Sthabar Jangam Achhe Yata,
Krishna Naam Diya Koilo Premete Unmatta.

(Ch.Ch. Madhya, Chap XVII)

Thereafter, he arrived at Kashi (Varanasi) and at the time of bathing in the Ganga at Monikornica Ghat met Sri Tapan Mishra whom he earlier during the tour of East Bengal advised to settle in Kashi and assured to meet him in future. Sri Tapan Mishra took Sri Chaitanyadeva at his residence. His son Raghu was given charge to serve him. Afterwards this Raghu was considered as one of the six Vaishnavas Bhatta Raghunath at Vrindaban. There another Sri Chandrasekhar in writing profession was engaged came to meet him. There he was initially not accepted by Sri Prakashananda a teacher in the Vedanta for his singing the Lord's name and dances. However, Sri Chaitanyadeva stayed at Sri Kashi Mishra's house for ten days. A Brahmin of Maharashtra became a devotee of him.

He came at Prayag and accordingly bathed in the water of three rivers' confluence. He stayed for three days here.

Thereafter, Sri Chaitanyadeva reached Mathura and bathed at the Bishranti Ghat in the Yamuna with joy for love of Sri Krishna. He visited the birth place of Keshav, Sri Krishna. Having seen the expression of love to Sri Krishna of Sri Chaitanyadeva all present were bewildered and one local Brahmin held the feet with deep respect. He also began to dance with Sri Chaitanyadeva in love to him as well as to Lord Sri Krishna. This old person was one of the disciples of Sripad Madhabendra Puri Sri Chaitanyadeva had special respect as also preceptor for him.

Sri Chaitanyadeva bathed at the twentyfour Ghats of the Yamuna. The twentyfour Ghats were:-

Abimukta, Bishranti, Guhya or Sansar Mochan, Prayag, Konkhol, Tinduk, Surya, Botaswami, Dhruba, Rishi, Moksha, Bodhi, Naba, Dharapatan, Sanjaman, Nag, Ghatavaran, Brahma, Som, Saraswati Tapan, Chakra, Dashaswamedh, Bigh Raj and Koti.

Here that old Brahmin as a guide took the charge to take Sri Chaitanyadeva to the pilgrims like Swambhu, Bishram, Dirgha Vishnu, Bhuteswar, Mahavidya, Gokarna and others. He also took him at Madhuban, Taal, Kumud, Bahula forests. Wherever Sri Chaitanyadeva went he took the holy bath with love for Sri Krishna Sri Chaitanyadeva was considered by all the Jibas in the forests of Mathura-Vrindaban as their friend. Love and love everywhere were found with the presence of Sri Chaitanyadeva.

Sahasra Guna Prem Barhe Mathura Darshane,
Laksha Guna Prem Barhe Bhrame Yabe Bone.

(Ch.Ch. Madhya, Chap XVII)

At Arit village Sri Chaitanyadeva asked about 'Radha Kunda' to all the persons he met even the company the old Brahmin failed to locate. At last with self realisation of the forgotton pilgrim Sri Chaitanyadeva started to take bath at two paddy fields and all the people there with the villagers were surprised to see him bathing in the water of the paddy fields. Sri Chaitanyadeva then began to praise Radha Kunda and thus the kunda was discovered by him. He also painted his whole body (Tilak) with the clay of the Kunda and Sri Balabhadra Bhattacharya took some clay with him.

Sri Chaitanyadeva visited with respect Harideva the Narayana in the village Gobardhan. He thought to himself, "I shall not climb on the hill Gobardhan". However, he could have darshan of Sri Gopal as He came down to His devotee.

Kabhu Kunje Rahe Kabhu Rahe Gramantare,
Sei Bhakta Tanha Aasi Dekhaye Tanhare.

(Ch.Ch. Madhya, Chap XVII)

Sri Chaitanyadeva visited Kamyabon, Nandishwar, the Cave, Khadir Bon, Leela Sthal, Srimati Laxmi, Sheshashayee, Bhanir Bon and crossing the Yamuna Bhadrabon and returning Louha Bon, the Birth Place and the places of Gokul. He reached Mathura and to avoid the crowd he went to Akrurtirtha. He bathed in the water of Kaliya Lake. He also bathed at Cheer Ghat in Vrindaban. He used to sing Harinaam under a tamarind tree near the Yamuna and beautiful scenery of Vrindaban. He remembered the Raasleela of Lord Sri Krishna and with attachment fainted.

There met Rajput Krishnadas with Sri Chaitanyadeva while he was advising all Harinaam Sankirtan. Sri Chaitanyadeva wherever went people from different places thronged there to have darshan of his divine look and sweet talks with Sankirtan and dances.

A rumour was there that Lord Sri Krishna has come to Mathura-Vrindaban but people who learnt it could not find Sri Krishna anywhere. People noticed that in the Lake of Kalidah a ray of light and a dancing figure of the snake Kaliya were seen at night. Having heard this Sri Balabhadra Bhattacharya also became interested to witness Sri Krishna and sought for permission from Sri Chaitanyadeva. In reply Sri Chaitanyadeva said - "Do not talk like an idiot. Alright, let me have exact information first. However, you may try to go tomorrow." Sri Chaitanyadeva thereafter came to know that a certain fisherman on a small boat and hanging a little lamp is fishing every night. The boat is swinging on the water of the lake and from the bank it looks that a ray of light and someone is dancing on the water. Sri Chaitanyadeva having known the fact explained to Balabhadra Bhattacharya and advised him to be practical. However, people began to say that Sri Chaitanyadeva was Sri Krishna or Sri Narayana. And day after day from morning to afternoon the gathering of visitors was increasing and sometime uncontrolable to the members of the accompanying team.

In order to avert the situation Sri Balabhadra Bhattacharya then humbly suggested Sri Chaitanyadeva to have holy bath in the Tribeni at Prayag at the full moon of the month of Magh. Sri Chaitanyadeva though did not want to leave Mathura-Vrindaban so early but could not dishearten Sri Balabhadra and after the bath in the Ganga at Sorakshetra in the district of Badao to the East side of Vrindaban began their return journey. Among the team Rajput Krishnadas and that old Brahmin were experts in guiding the route of travel along the Ganga.

On the way Sri Chaitanyadeva hearing someone to play in flute became fainted in love of Lord Sri Krishna. A team of ten Pathaan armed cavalrymen were passing through the path and found a person with saffron dress was lying on the shore and some people were guarding him. They came to them and had the doubt that these people would rob the unconscious man. They were to kill the men with their sword. But Rajput Krishnadas requested them to wait and see the fact. All were tied with ropes by them and began to wait for return of consciousness of Sri Chaitanyadeva. After some time Sri Chaitanyadeva getting consciousness rose and sat on the shore. Among the horsemen one was like a Peer having some knowledge in religion wanted to ask some questions to testify Sri Chaitanyadeva. Sri Chaitanyadeva was not a person to fail in debates. Ultimately he won and all the Pathaans then bowed their heads at the feet of Sri Chaitanyadeva and they wanted to follow the Vaishnavism. The Peer like horseman was named as Ramdas and another was named as Bijuli Khan. All are called Pathaan Vaishnavas.

Thereafter, Sri Chaitanyadeva and his team restarted to return towards Prayag.

Sri Roop

Sri Chaitanyadeva lived on Tribeni at Prayag for some days at the residence of earlier known Brahmin of South India. There came up Sri Roop and his brother Ballav (Anupam) from Goud. Sri Chaitanyadeva was pleased to receive them. He knew that their elder brother Sri Sanatan remained as captive in Goud. He knows everything and informed them that in the mean time Sri Sanatan having left bondage was coming nearer. The two brothers here also arranged their residence in order to stay nearer to their Sri Chaitanya Mahaprabhu. On hearing learned Sri Ballav Bhatta came and invited Sri Chaitanyadeva to his residence at Arail Village off Prayag. There came another learned Vaishnava from Mithila Sri Raghupati Upadhyay. He bowed his head at the feet of Sri Chaitanyadeva. He recited different Shlokas on Lord Sri Krishna to Sri Chaitanyadeva. One of the Shlokas was:-

"Out of the various images the blackish image is the best. Out of various places of His stay Braja Dham is the best. Out of different age groups adolescene group is the best and out of various flavours the flavour of eternal love's ultimate union is the best."

Shyamameba Parang Rupang Puri Madhupuri Bora,
Bayah Koishorakang Dhyeyamadya Eba Paro Rasah.
(Ch.Ch. Madhya, Chap XIX)

Thereafter, Sri Chaitanyadeva in order to avoid much crowd selected **'Dashaswamedh Ghat'** and there he induced strength in Sri Roop to accept what he would coach. Sri Chaitanyadeva then days after days taught him **Krishna Tattwa, Bhakti Tattwa, Rausa Tattwa, Bhagawata Tattwa** etc.

Lok Bhir Bhaye Prabhu Dashaswamedhe Jaiya,
Roop Gossainke Shiksha Karan Shakti Sanchariya,
Krishna Tattwa, Bhakti Tattwa, Rausa Tattwa Pranta,
Sob Shikhailo Prabhu Bhagawata Siddhanta.
... ...
Sri roop Hridayae Prabhu Shakti Sancharilo,
Sarba Tattwa Nirupane Pravin Karila.
(Ch.Ch. Madhya, Chap XIX)

Sri Chaitanyadeva then advised Sri Roop and Sri Ballav that now they should go to Vrindaban and then from Goud they might meet him at Neelachal. The sesson took only ten days to equip Sri Roop as he narrated all the Tattwa in short.

Thus, Sri Roop became vast knowledgeable and as an expertised in taking all the decisions on Vaishnavism and with the permission of Sri Chaitanya Mahaprabhu went to Vrindaban.

Sri Roop Goswami (1489 - 1564/65 AD) afterwards authored the books like **'Hansadot', 'Uddhav Sandesh', 'Daankeli Koumudi', 'Vaktirasamrita Sindhu', 'Ujjwal Nilmoni', 'Laghu Ganoddesh Deepika', 'Bidagdha Madhav', 'Lalit Madhav', 'Gangastakam'** etc.

In the beginning during the Nabadwip Lila Sri Gourangadeva had already sent the people like Sri Bhugarva Goswami and Sri Lokenath Goswami and, thereafter, also Sri Subuddhi Roy to Vrindaban for revival of abandoned deities and temples in Vrindaban. He also advised Sri Subuddhi Roy to please look after any inconvenience of the poor devotees in Vrindaban.

Sri Chaitanya Mahaprabhu taught not only Sri Roop he also taught his brother Anupam and embraced both of them. He, afterwards, lessoned Sri Sanatan for two months living at the house of Sri Chandrasekhar. Then he used to receive alms at the house of Sri Tapan Mishra. Kavi Karnapur in his writings have discussed all the facts relating to the teachings to Sri Roop and Sri Sanatan.

Eimata Karnapur Likhe Sthane Sthane,
Prabhu Kripa Koilo Joichhe Roop-Sanatane.
(Ch.Ch. Madhya, Chap XIX)

Sri Chaitanya Mahaprabhu used to ask all the devotees who occasionally visited Vrindaban how his beloved Sri Roop and Sri Sanatan and other Vaishnavas were living in Vrindaban. He was also satisfied to learn that they were the icons of sacrifice. They did not bother about their shelter, rather they preferred under any tree and on the bricks as pillows to pass the night. They lived on alms whatever those were like dried Rooti or dried peas etc.

Bipra Grihe Sthul Viksha, Kanha Madhukari,
Sushka Rooti Chana Chabaya Bhog Parihari.
Karoya Matra Hathe Kantha Chhirah Bahirbaas,
Krishna Katha, Krishna Naam, Nartan Ullas.
Astaprahara Krishna-Bhajan Chari Danda Shayane
Naam Sankirtan Seho Nahe Kono Dine.
Kabhu Bhaktirasa Shastra Karaye Likhan,
Chaitanya Katha Shune, Kare Chaitana-Chintan.
(Ch.Ch. Madhya, Chap XVII)

Thereafter, Sri Chaitanyadeva reached Varanasi and Sri Chandrasekhar took him with others at his residence. Came Sri Tapan Mishra there and arranged the alms at his residence. People, mainly the elites from different places began to come and meet Sri Chaitanyadeva.

Sri Sanatan

Thereafter **Sri Sanatan** after fleeing by giving bribe of seven thousand from captivity of Hussein Shah in disguise of a Faquir could reach Varanasi and sat at the door of Sri Chandrasekhar wherein Sri Chaitanyadeva was residing. Sri Chaitanyadeva feeling his presence advised Sri Chandrasekhar to bring the Faquir inside. Sri Chaitanyadeva embraced Sri Sanatan with immense love.

With necessary advice by Sri Chaitanyadeva Sri Chandrasekhar arranged to refresh Sri Sanatan and thereafter, at the residence of Tapan Mishra he did not wear the new dress offered by Sri Tapan Mishra but took an old used cloth. The company Brahmin of Maharastra also after being introduced wished to give him alms for the days of his stay too but Sri Sanatan refused to take alms at one place for several days as an ascetic or Vaishnava should not do. Door to door begging is the best for him, he stated.

Sri Chaitanyadeva having known the sacrifice and also observed him here a real Vaishnava as he dreamt of was highly pleased. However, Sri Chaitanyadeva was repeatedly staring at the blanket what on way his brother-in-law at Hazipur feeling the cold forcedly gifted him. Sri Sanatan could get that this blanket was not a choice of Sri Chaitanyadeva. He went at the nearest Ghat of the Ganga and found a goudiya who set his cotton wrapper for drying in the sun. He requested the person to give him the wrapper in lieu of the blanket he wore. The person was surprised but could not stop Sri Sanatan from taking it in lieu of the blanket. To find wearing the ordinary cotton wrapper Sri Chaitanyadeva was highly satisfied.

Eta Boli Kantha Loilo Bhot Tare Diya,
Gossainr Thai Aaila Kantha Gale Diya,
Prabhu Kahe Tomar Bhot-Kambal Kotha Gelo ,
Prabhupade Sob Katha Gossain Kahilo,
Prabhu Kahe Iha Aami Kariyachhi Bichar,
Bishayabhog Khandailo Krishna Ye Tomar.

(Ch.Ch. Madhya, Chap XX)

Sri Chaitanya Mahaprabhu took almost two months for teaching the Tattwas to Sri Sanatan at the Ghat days after days.

Sanatan Gossain Aasi Tnahai Milila,
Tnar Shiksha Lagi Prabhu Du Mas Rahila.

(Ch.Ch.Adi, Chap IX)

Sri Sanatan Goswami (1480/88 - 1558/1565 AD) afterwards authored the books like **'Brihad Bhagawatamrita', 'Digdarshini Tika', 'Lila Stab or Dasham Charitra', 'Dasham Tippani or Vaishnavatoshini'** and edited the most important scripture **'Haribhakti Vilas'** prepared by Sri Gopal Bhatta.

After equipping with the scriptures referring the Srimad Vagawata, Srimad Bhagawatageeta, Sri Hari Bhakti Vilas, Sri Vishnu Purana, Laghu Bhagawatamrita, Brahma Sanhita and others to Sri Roop and Sri Sanatan Sri Chaitanya Mahaprabhu decided to return to Neelachal via Jharikhand.

Sri Chaitanyadeva also sang the Kirtan and danced in love for Lord Sri Krishna and hundreds of people including Vedantik Prakashananda Saraswati who at first did not prefer to care Sri Chaitanya Mahaprabhu for his own ego of wisdom in the Vedanta-Upanishads now apologized for his previous misbehave. Sri Chaitanya Mahaprabhu received him by embracing. Sri Prakashananda was related with Sri Gopal Bhatta whom Sri Chaitanyadeva met at his teens during the last South India Tour at Srirangam in the house of Sri Venkata Bhatta. Sri Gopal Bhatta and Prakashananda Saraswati both were from the house of Sri Venkata Bhatta of Srirangam.

Sri Chaitanya Mahaprabhu sang and danced nicely for unconditional love to Sri Krishna.

Hari Haraye Namah Krishna Yadabaya Namah,
Gopala Govinda Rama Sri Madhusudana.

(Ch.Ch. Adi, Chap. VII)

পুরীতে নরেন্দ্র-সরোবরতীরে সপরিকর শ্রীশ্রীচৈতন্যদেব শ্রীগদাধর মুখে ভাগবত পাঠ শ্রবণ করছেন

প্রায় পাঁচশত বৎসরের প্রাচীন এই ঐতিহাসিক চিত্রটি উড়িষ্যার মহারাজা প্রতাপরুদ্র চৈতন্যদেবের প্রকটকালেই কোন শিল্পীকে দিয়ে অঙ্কিত করিয়েছিলেন। চৈতন্যদেবের দেহাবসানের পর বিরহাকুল শ্রীনিবাস আচার্যকে পরে এই চিত্র উপহৃত হয়। শ্রীনিবাস আচার্যের বংশধর শ্রীল রাধামোহন ঠাকুর উক্ত চিত্রখানি তাঁহার শিষ্য মহারাজ নন্দকুমারকে উপহার দেন। তদবধি এই চিত্র মুর্শিদাবাদে নন্দকুমারের প্রাসাদ — কুঞ্জঘাটা রাজবাটিতে সযত্নে রক্ষিত আছে বলে জানা যায়।
(শ্রীশ্রীচৈতন্যদেব গ্রন্থ থেকে)

Return from Mathura-Vrindaban at Narendra Sarobar in Puri

Ultimately Sri Chaitanyadeva returned via Jharikhanda and reached near Narendra Sarobar in Neelachal. There thousands of devotees assembled and started singing Harinaam Sankirtan to receive him warmly. And as inspired by Sri Chaitanyadeva all the associates and the devotees began to play with the water of the Sarobar. All sprayed water to each other without any discrimination. The bank of Narendra got shape of a big conference. Sri Chaitanyadeva considered the Sarobar as pious like the Ganga and the Yamuna.

At last in the afternoon Sri Gadadhara Pundit in melodious voice read and elucidated sweetly the Srimad Bhagawata to Sri Chaitanyadeva and the thousands of devotees and associates. So, Narendra Sarobar became a historic place.

Ballav Bhatta in Puri

Once, Sri Ballav Bhatta from Arail Village near Prayag came to Neelachal-Puri to meet Sri Chaitanyadeva.

The exceptionally learned Sri Ballav Bhatta was a vedantic scholar. He was of Bharadwaj Gotra under Taittariya branch of Yayurveda. His parents Sri Laxman and Srimati Ballamagaru from Andhra Pradesh came to Varanasi and lived at Hanuman Ghat of Kashidham. Once by hearing a rumour that Kashidham would be attacked and plundered by a group of Muslim soldiers they began to flee through the dense forests towards their native village in Andhra Pradesh. At that time mother Srimati Ballamagaru was carrying. On way of fleeing through the forests of Champaran (Raipur) in Madhya Pradesh Srimati Ballamagaru due to labour pain was ultimately foced to give birth of a male child. Thus, Sri Ballav Bhatta was born in Baishakh (April-May) in 1479 AD. Afterwards when normalcy was restored Sri Laxman Bhatta with his family returned Varanasi.

Sri Ballav Bhatta learnt various scriptures on Hindu Philosophy from Yoti in Varanasi. Later in the South he defeated logically the 'Mayavad' in a debate and he could easily establish the 'Shuddhawitabad'. He was awarded with the Title 'Acharya' by the eminent scholar Sri Vyastirtha in the court of the King of Vijaynagar. In his lifetime he travelled at almost the whole of India thrice. After marriage he considered not to dwell and maintain family life in the holy place of Shiva Mahadeva Varanasi and chose to settle at Arail Village near Prayag. He also worked on the Upanishads, the Srimad Bhagawata and the Brahma Sutra.

Once, during the stayal from Mathura-Vrindaban to Puri of Sri Chaitanyadeva at Prayag invited him at his residence at Arail and with Sri Raghupati Upadhyay of Mithila they passed the days in festivity in divinely atmosphere accompanied with dances and Harinaam Sankirtan.

After a couple of years Sri Ballav Bhatta arrived at Puri to visit Sri Chaitanyadeva and his associations there. He also had written some Shlokas praising Sri Chaitanyadeva and a Note on the Srimad Bhagawata. He wished to read the Note to Sri Chaitanyadeva. But Sri Chaitanyadeva found that there were some deviations from the mostly preferred by Vaishnavas the Tika of Srimad Bhagawata by Sridharswami as running. He, therefore, refused to listen to the Note and rebuked him much. So, being morose Sri Ballav Bhatta went from one door to another door if anyone listens to his Note but each and everyone refused to read or listen to it as Sri Chaitanyadeva refused to listen to.

One day, Sri Ballav Bhatta found Sri Gadadhar Pundit to come to Gambhira very politely. He observed minutely Sri Gadadhar Pundit and was highly attracted for the qualities of loyalty, sincerety, humbleness, virtuous practices etc. he decided to read his Note to Sri Gadadhar Pundit who hardly refuses anybody and agreed to listen to it. At Tota where Sri Sri Gopinathji was worshipped by Sri Gadadhar Pundit Sri Ballav Bhatta began to read his Note. Sri Gadadhar Pundit once asked whether the same was brought to the notice of Sri Chaitanyadeva. Sri Ballav Bhatta, in reply described the matter that already happened to him. Sri Gadadhar Pundit said that he only knew the preference of Sri Chaitanyadeva. He is God as well as Lord Sri Krishna or Lord Gopinathji to him.

Sri Gadadhar Pundit calmly told Sri Ballav Bhatta - "No Sir, without his approval I can not think otherwise even I cannot breathe at all."

Sri Ballav Bhatta, a man of quality, was so surprised to note the love and sincerety of Sri Gadadhar Pundit that his respect for him enhanced.

One day at an invitation party of Harinaam Sankirtan and after taking Prasad at the place of Sri Jagadananda, Sri Ballav Bhatta sought for approval of Sri Chaitanyadeva that he intended to take initiation in Sri Krishna mantra from Sri Gadadhar Pundit. Sri Chaitanyadeva was pleased to learn it and there he advised Sri Gadadhar Pundit to do the needful accordingly.

Sri Ballav Bhatta was earlier initiated in Gopal mantra and now having been initiated in the mantra of Lord Sri Krishna from Sri Gadadhar Pundit realised the 'Madhur Rasa' the love for God. Thus, Sri Ballav Bhatta could leave all the egos, pride for his wisdom and like a modest Vaishnava returned to his Arail Village near Prayag. Thousands of his disciples already knew him as Ballavacharya and they remained in worshipping Lord Gopal.

Kavi Karnapur described him as Sri Sukhdeva. Sri Ballavacharya or Sri Ballav Bhatta had written the explanatory note as Subodhini on Sri Mad Bhagawata and other scriptures.

According to Dr. Biman Behari Majumder has commented that Sri Ballav Bhatta or Sri Ballavacharya was renowned personality in the Northern India.

In the 'Sri Ballavacharyajiki Nijabarta' published from Veer Vijoy Press of Ahmedabad and the 'Sampradaya Pradipe' published from Kankroli Vidya Vivag also admitted that Sri Chaitanyadeva once visited him at Arail Village near Prayag off Varanasi.

According to Dr. Sarvapalli Radhakrishnan, Ballabha is a Telegu Brahmin of South India who migrated to the north and developed the views of Vishnusawmin, who belonged to the thirteenth century. He accepts the authority not only of Upanishadas, the Bhagavadgita and the Brahma-sutra, but also of the Bhagabat Purana. In his works Anubhasya, Siddhantarahasya and Bhagabattika Sibodhini, he offers a theistic interpretation of the Vedanta, which differs from those of Sankara and Ramanuja.

(Indian Philosophy
by Dr. Sarvapalli Radhakrishnan, Vol - II)

Correction of Diksha Mantra of Gadadhara Pundit

Somehow Sri Gadadhar Pundit forgot to remember the exact wordings of his mantra received in initiation properly. Perhaps he had mistakenly disclosed his own mantra to other or at the time of initiation to other disciples. So, the mantra needed for correction from the Preceptor, if he is available or alive or from a respectable person who can be a Preceptor. Sri Gadadhar Pundit approached Sri Chaitanyadeva for necessary correction. He was always ready to consider him as the Preceptor.

Sri Chaitanyadeva thought for sometime and answered - Do not worry my dear Gadadhara. Your own Preceptor Sri Pundarik Vidyanidhi is still alive."

Sri Gadadhar Pundit replied - "May be so but I do not know where he is now. I feel helpless and you are only here who can do the necessary correction, Mahaprabhu please do not hesitate."

Sri Chaitanyadeva thought again for a few seconds and replied - "I said to you your own Preceptor Sri Pundarik Vidyanidhi is still alive and after travelling many places he is now coming towards Neelachal. See, he is coming here within ten days."

Sri Gadadhar Pundit became calm as the words spoken by his best friend Sri Chaitanyadeva cannot be a false assurance.

In fact, within ten days Sri Pundarik Vidyanidhi arrived at Neelachal to see Sri Sri Jagannatha Mahaprabhu and also to meet Sri Chaitanyadeva and others there. Both Sri Chaitanyadeva and Sri Pundarik Vidyanidhi greeted each other by embracing. Tears in love for God Sri Sri Jagannatha Mahaprabhu and Sri Krishna from their eyes dropped for some time. Thereafter, Sri Pundarik Vidyanidhi duly corrected the Diksha Mantra to Sri Gadadhar Pundit.

He was also an earlier friend to Sri Swarup Damodar and he stayed in Puri for several days with him.

Sri Raghunath Das Goswami

The author of Sri Chaitanyacharitamrita has elaborately discussed on Sri Raghunathdas the son Sri Gobardhandas Majumdar of Saptagram in the district of Hooghly. He being a Non-Brahmin Kayaystha was awarded the title of Goswami for his deep devotion to Lord Sri Krishna and Sri Chaitanyadeva. He was Rasamanjari in his earlier life. Some indicated him as Bhanumati in earlier life also.

Sri Hiranya Majumdar and Sri Gobardhandas Majumdar were two brothers having annual income more than twenty lakhs out of which they had to hand over twelve lakhs of Rupees to the then Ruler of Goud Bengal.

Sri Raghunathdas loved Sri Chaitanyadeva much. After the Sannyas while Sri Chaitanyadeva was in Shantipur at the house of Sri Adwaita Acharya he met him and informed him that he had no attraction in family life and wanted to take Sannyas. He stayed there for five to seven days.

There once lived Sri Haridas who used to utter Sri Harinaam for three lakhs a day at the house of Sri Balaram Pundit at Chandapur near Saptagram. Sri Balaram Pundit was the priest at the temple of the Majumdar family. So, Sri Raghunathdas had the opportunity to have contacts with Sri Haridas easily and became fond of Sri Chaitanyadeva.

Sri Raghunath Das was a disciple Sri Jadunandan Acharya who was one of the disciple of Sri Adwaita Acharya.

Once he was confined in the jail of the then representative of Yaban Ruler as his father and the uncle were not found at their Home for the charge of not paying Ruler's tax what they were appointed to collect from the traders and the cultivators and others in the area. Raghunath then could easily make understand the Ruler that it was not praiseworthy for him to torture who is like a son. He also called him as a 'Jinda Peer'. The Ruler having noticed the pure and innocent face of Raghunath could not hurt him on the condition to bring his father and the elder uncle what he humbly agreed to. Lastly the matter was solved that annual income from the tax more than twenty lakhs out of which they would hand over twelve lakhs of Rupees to the Ruler.

Thus, almost two years were passed. He again wanted to leave the family bondage. His elder uncle and father could catch him with the people of their estate and tried to confine him in a room. He was also caused to marry a beautiful girl. But he was like a bird who flies in the blue sky with freedom.

He wanted to meet Sri Chaitanyadeva while after Ramkeli on way to return to Neelachal was in Shantipur at the house of Sri Adwaita Acharya. With humble and repeated requests his parents and the elder uncle allowed him with eleven escorts and huge materials. This was the second time that he could see Sri Chaitanyadeva and remained there for seven days. Ultimately, Sri Chaitanyadeva advised him:-

Markat Boiragya Na Kara Lok Dekhaiya,
Jathajogya Bishaya Bhunja Anasakta Hoinya.
Antara Nishtha Kara Bahye Lok Byabahara,
Achirate Krishna Tomay Kariben Uddhara.

(Krishnadas Kaviraj Sri Ch. Ch.Madhya, Chap XVI)

Afterwards getting news that Sri Chaitanyadeva from Mathura-Vrindaban tour returned to Neelachal, Sri Raghunathadas became almost mad to meet Sri Chaitanyadeva. But he was under a strict surveillance with escort armed with 'lathi'.

In the mean time, Sri Raghunathadas got the information that Sri Nityananda an important associate of Sri Chaitanyadeva has arrived at the house of Sri Raghav Pundit at Panihati and staying there. He hurriedly reached at the ghat of Panihati and met Sri Nityanandaprabhu. Among the huge number of people who were surrounding he bowed his head from a distance. Sri Nityanandaprabhu took him up and said:-

... ...Chora Dili Darshan,
Aaya Aaya Aaj Tor Karimu Dandan.
(Krishnadas Kaviraj Sri Ch. Ch. Antya, Chap VI)

As a punishment for meeting Sri Chaitanyadeva twice in Shantipur imposed by Sri Nityanandaprabhu was nothing but to feed Chida (pressed rice), Curd, Banana, Mango and sweets to all the people came from different places and different castes in the mid of the day. Sri Raghunathadas gladly arranged the food for hundreds of the crowd. And, afterwards, he sought for permission from Sri Nityanandaprabhu to meet Sri Chaitanyadeva in Neelachal.

Tomar Kripa Bina Keha Chaitanya Nahi Paay,
Tumi Kripa Koile Tare Adhameha Paay.
Ajogya Mui, Nibedan Karite Karon Bhoy,
More Chaitanya Deha Gossain! Hoiya Saday.
(Krishnadas Kaviraj Sri Ch. Ch. Antya, Chap VI)

From that day Sri Raghunathadas did not sleep inside the bed room at the house of Saptagram. He stayed outside of the house at 'Durga Mandap' but the people of his escort were there for watch sleeplessly so that Sri Raghunathadas could not flee. By chance, one day at the ending of the night his preceptor Sri Jadunandan Acharya came there and requested him to make agree his another Brahmin disciple who was given the charge of service in the family temple for cooking and servicing and also worshipping the deity but he was not coming for some days. Sri Raghunathadas remembered the words once spoken by Sri Chaitanyadeva that:-

"Achirate Krishna Tomay Karibe Udhwar

(Krishnadas Kaviraj Sri Ch. Ch.Madhya, Chap XVI)

He looked at the escort persons and was confirmed that in the early morning's mild sweet air they could not resist sleeping. They all were sleeping and Sri Raghunath began to walk with Sri Jadunandan Acharya and in the mid-way he bowed his head to the Preceptor and said to him that such an old person as Sri Jadunandan Acharya need not go alongwith him and he would convince the priest to attend the temple otherwise in want of capable Brahmin the worshipping of the deity would be suspended.

Sri Jadunandan Acharya naturally blessed him by saying "God would fulfill his desire."

Sri Raghunathadas hurriedly managed to escape from family life. He did not follow the regular route of Vaishnavas from Bengal to Odisha and walked speedily through uncommon roads full of bushes and thorns. The people of Sri Gobardhandas and Sri Hiranyadas ran in search of him but he was not found in the team of Sri Shibananda Sen. Without any stop for having no food he could reach within only twelve days much before the party of Sri Shibananda Sen reached at Puri, He ate only three days while walking. He was full of dust and weak when he reached at the feet of Sri Chaitanyadeva.

He easily left behind his beautiful and young wife. He was so respected by all the Vaishnavas and the associates of Sri Chaitanyadeva. Sri Chaitanyadeva in Neelachal kept him under the care of Sri Swarup Damodar and gave his company all the time. Thus, Sri Raghunath became a Vaishnava Sadhak and later a prominent leader of the Vaishnavas. His sacrifice was so acute that once he received the Prasad what Sri Govinda used bring from the Temple of Jagannathaswami and it continued only for three days.

Afterwards, Sri Raghunath used to collect Prasad at queue of the begging persons. But after a few days he also left the daily routine of waiting for Prasad in the line. He then used to take the Prasad what were left in the drain. He used to wash the dirty things from the Prasad and used to receive with some salt. Sri Chaitanyadeva also took by force from him such Prasad and called it as nector. But Sri Swarup Damodar could not allow him to have such Prasad.

Sri Swarup Damodar sufficiently educated Sri Raghunathdas and Sri Chaitanyadeva wanted to teach all others what maximum the apathy towards earthly materials and pleasure could be. He advised him to take Harinaam all the time, have minimum pure and simple food and simple living, not to indulge greed of human beings any kind.

"Bhalo Na Khaibey Bhalo Na Peribey".

and

"Boiragi Karibe Sada Naam Samkirtan."

Sri Chaitanyadeva also advised him:-

Amani Mana Dena Krishna Naam Sada Labe,
Braje Radhakrishna Seva Manase Kribe.

(Ref. Krishnadas Kaviraj Sri Ch. Ch. Antya 6/234)

Sri Chaitanyadeva gifted him with 'Gunja Mala', without any confusion and a piece of stone of Gobardhan Hill and advised him to consider it as Lord Sri Krishna. One of the followers of Sri Raghunath Das Goswami purchased the land at Radha Kunda and Shyam Kunda and at his own renovated them.

Sri Raghunathdas was sent to Vrindaban taking with all the writings of Sri Chaitanyadeva, Sri Raghunathdas and his own notings before the disappearances of Sri Chaitanyadeva with Sri Gadadhara Pundit and the sudden death of Sri Swarup Damodar.

Being Inspired and supplied some information by Raghunath Das Goswami Krishnadas Kaviraj has composed the Sri Sri Chaitanya Charitamrita and got initiation and teachings from him.

Sri Raghunathdas Goswami has written 'Stababoli', 'Daan Charit', 'Mukta Charit' etc. poems and poetic drama. His sacrifice was beyond imagination and Sadhana was also to be remembered by all the Vaishnavas. He was exactly an icon of Bairagi of Goudiya Vaishnavas.

VIII. The Rathayatra

Goudiya Vaishnavas in Neelachal 2nd Time

In 1435 Shaka before the 2nd Ratha Yatra of the presence of Sri Chaitanyadeva the Goudiya Vaishnavas and their wives all assembled in Neelachal to witness the Mega Ratha Yatra of Lord Jagannath in the month of Ashada. The women of Goud Bengal brought with them various commodities of food stuff and spices for their beloved Sri Nemai.

Sri Shibananda Sen was the organiser of the tour for the people of Goud Bengal. He as a guide takes the pilgrims towards Neelachal and arranges the temporary residences there for their stayal. Sri Nityanandaprabhu, although was advised not to come Neelachal every year, in love of Sri Chaitanyadeva joined the team of the pilgrims.

Once during the stayal the wife of Sri Adwaita Acharya and Srimati Sitadevi cooked various items. Sri Adwaita Acharya an expert in cooking also participated with his wife. They both wanted to feed Sri Chaitanyadeva alone. In the Leelas Sri Chaitanyadeva would visit everywhere with one or more companies as he could not stop anyone or to say to allow him to remain alone. So the spouses were anxious how Sri Chaitanyadeva would come to their residence alone in the midday. All on a sudden a storm with heavy shower the roads became impassable. And so no one of the associates could reach him and Sri Chaitanyadeva alone started to walk alone in the storm and heavy shower but these could not harm him and he reached the residence of Sri Adwaita Acharya Srimati Sitadevi. Sri Adwaita Acharya thanked Devraj Indra for his mercy on him. Srimati Sitadevi with full satisfaction fed Prasad their beloved Sri Gouranga. Sri Adwaita Acharya at 80 had some secret matter to discuss with Sri Chaitanyadeva. What was the topic still remains secret.

Hari Hare Yeno Teno Chaitanya Adwaita.

(Ch.Bh. Antya, Chap 8)

In the Rathayatra with Sri Adwaita Acharya Sri Swaroop Damodar, Sri Gadadhara Pundit, Sri Nityanandaprabhu and thousands of devotees and Kirtaniyas Sri Chaitanyadeva sang and danced in love of Lord

Jagannathadeva. He was becoming absorbed in the singing and dancing madly at the centres of the seven teams of Kirtaniyas at a time. Among all the teams each team could see that Sri Chaitanyadeva was only with them. This was also witnessed by the King and Sri Sarbabhouma Bhattacharya.

All after the Rathayatra and 'Chaturmasya' began to return Goud Bengal. Sri Chaitanyadeva had tears in the eyes, while by embracing gave them goodbye personally citing the names of each person. He knew all of them as his own relatives.

Sri Chaitanyadeva on the next day expressed his desire to Sri Nityanandaprabhu by saying again that Sri Nityanadaprabhu need not be present in Neelachal every year. He requested that the tough work of spreading Harinaam to all irrespective of caste or any differences to be shouldered by Sri Nityanandaprabhu in his absence in Goud Bengal.

Bakreswar Pundit

Sri Bakreswar Pundit whose brilliant dances with Kirtan was preferred by Sri Chaitanyadeva. He believed "Bakreswar-Hridaye-Krishna Nija Ghar". He was one of the few selected disciples of Sri Gadadhar Pundit. He also remained unmarried like his Preceptor. He was included in one of the teams of seven circles of singers at the front of Rathayatra. In the circle wherein the then famous singer Sri Govinda Ghose who was leading the Kirtan Sri Bakreswar Pundit danced marvellously hours after hours. There were also the two brothers Sri Madhab and Sri Basudeva also joined. Sri Vishnudas and Sri Haridas also were welcomed to sing but Sri Bakreswar Pundit remained dancing all the way of the Rathayatra. His disciple was Sri Devananda Pundit whom Sri Chaitanyadeva advised to narrate the Sri Mad Bhagawata not only with the grammar but also with 'Bhakti'. He had another noted disciple Sri Gopal Guru.

Sri Gopal Guru

Sri Gopal Guru was then younger one. He was earlier known as Sri Makardhwaz Pundit. On initiation from Sri Bakreswar Pundit he was named as 'Manju medhika'.

There is an amusing story known by many of the devotees about the naming Gopal Guru by Sri Chaitanyadeva. As one of the direct followers of Sri Chaitanyadeva he took up from very childhood some essential services to him. It is heard that one day in an early in the morning while Sri Chaitanyadeva was engaged to empty the bowels on a field as usual he was waiting with a water pot for him and he noticed that Sri Chaitanyadeva remained silent. He was accustomed to hear the Sri Krishna naam all the time in the lips of Sri Chaitanyadeva. It made him surprised. Afterwards, he asked Sri Chaitanyadeva - "Prabhu I am surprised to note that I have not heard any sound of your uttering the name of Sri Krishna while you were ...is there any reason behind this unusual happenning?"

Actually Sri Chaitanyadeva locked his tongue and remained without the name of Lord Sri Krishna, what he usually does not. He was pleased to hear it. To his query he answered - "Thank you Gopal. You are right. Not a single moment should be left without Harinaam Gopal. You are like a Guru to me. From today you would be called Gopal Guru."

Sri Gopal Guru by caste Brahmin born in whose actual name was Makardhwaj Pundit. He was son of Murari Pundit. From very childhood started to serve Sri Chaitanyadeva. He was called as Gopal later Mahaprabhu Sri Chaitanyadeva adding the word 'Guru' called him as 'Gopal Guru'. Writtings were 'Smaran Karma Paddhati' and 'Seva Smaran Paddhati'. He was given the charge of the responsibility of serving 'Gour Gambhira' after Bakreswar Pundit. He also established the deity of Radhakanta and Mutt in Puri. There are eight Mutts of them in Odisha.

Goudiya Vaishnavas in Neelachal 3rd Time

In 1436 Shaka before the 3rd Ratha Yatra the devotees from Goud Bengal came to Neelachal and Sri Shibananda Sen was the organiser of the tour.

With the attraction of Sri Chaitanyadeva Sri Nityanandaprabhu could not obey the request of Sri Chaitanyadeva and having permission from Sachimaa at Nabadwip came to Neelachal with the Gopals and along with the 'Raghavera Jhali' prepared by Dayamantidevi, sister of Raghav Pundit.

He entered Kamalpur and in a flower garden began to meditate and was waiting for Sri Chaitanyadeva. On the other hand, Sri Chaitanyadeva at Gambhira, understanding without any source that Nityanandaprabhu's coming himself advanced at the garden to receive Sri Nityanandaprabhu. After having cordially received Sri Nityanandaprabhu visited Sri Sri Jagannathadeva and went to Sri Gadadhara Pundit at Tota. Sri Nityanandaprabhu had immense affection and love for Pundit Gadadhara as he was the most beloved by Sri Chaitanyadeva from their childhood. He was highly welcomed by Pundit. He also brought one maund fine rice and coloured dress for Sri Sri Gopinath at Tota. Gadadhara cooked with the rice and some vegetables including some leaves of tamarind from the adjacent garden. While then the offering to Lord Gopinath Sri Gadadhara was in thought of Sri Chaitanyadeva, Both of them Netai-Gadadhara, were almost ready to have the Prasad.

At that time with smiles in face Sri Chaitanyadeva reached there and said:-

Haasiya Bolen Prabhu, Shuno Gadadhara,
Aami Ki Na Hoi Nimantranera Bhitara,
Aamito Tomra Dui Hoite Bhinna Noi,
Na Dileo Tomra Balete Aami Loi.

(Ch. Bh. Antya, Chap 7)

Both Sri Gadadhara Pundit and Sri Nityananda became surprised and they highly pleased to have company of their mostly wanted Sri Chaitanyadeva. The limit of their happiness could not be measured. Sri Chaitanyadeva smilingly again said to lifelong friend Gadadhara Pundit:-

Ni tyananda Drabya Gopinthera Prasad,
Tomara Randhan Mor Ithe Aachhe Bhaag.

(Ch.Bh.Antya, Chap 7)

The trio sat and began to receive Prasad. Sri Chaitanyadeva as usual practice started to praise the Prasad as well as the cooking of Sri Gadadhara Pundit. More over he used to see Gadadhara as Srimati Radharani of Braja who had only one ambition to please Sri Krishna.

The trio, however, there for the period remained along:-

Henamate Nityananda Prabhu Neelachale
Biharena Gourachandra Sange Kutuhale,
Tinjan Ekatra Thaken Nirantara,
Sri Krishna Chaitanya Nityananda Gadadhara.

(Ch.Bh. Antya, Chap 7)

Since in 1442 Shaka (1520 AD) the information of the Rathayatra wherein Sri Chaitanyadeva was present till 1455 Shaka (1533 AD) are not easily available by a tiny writer like me.

Teachings by Lifestyle

He did not prefer luxurious life for a Sannyasi or Bairagi to enjoy. One day Jagananda, engaged in looking after the external affairs, took some oil from Sri Sibananda Sen of Bengal and prepared of sandalwood scented oil for Sri Chaitanyadeva and gave it to Sri Govinda who used to look after the personal matters of Sri Chaitanyadeva. Govinda informed Sri Chaitanyadeva but he replied it would be better for lighting the lamps of Sri Sri Jagannathprabhu.

On another day Govinda reminded Sri Chaitanyadev that the oil may help to keep head cool and it may also help sound sleep at night. Sri Chaitanyadeva replied that he has not taken the life of a Sannyasi (mendicant) for a luxurious life to enjoy. Sri Jagadananda was aggrieved and threw the pitcher full of scented oil on the courtyard. Then Sri Jagadananda entered his room and having it locked remained without taking any food for consecutive three days. Sri Chaitanyadeva on hearing this, reached at his residence and requested him to break the fasting, as Sri Chaitanyadeva would receive Prasad at his place. That was the feeling for an associate who was somehow hurt.

Once Sri Chaitanyadeva advised Sri Raghunathdas Goswami and all others to lead simple life and not to consume rich and costly food and in much quantity and to wear rich dresses.

Sri Chaitanyadeva himself also preferred to get Prasad of simple rice and lafra (one type curry of mixed vegetables) and distribute the delicious Prasad to other followers accompanied him.

Not to Cross Limit

One day, Sri Sanatan after coming to Neelachal expressed to Sri Jagadananda his hesitation that he perhaps is a leper and so, he should not mix the devotees in Puri. Sri Sanatan actually was affected by skin disease due to taking drinking water at the time of his journey through Jharikhand. It seemed to him to be disease Leprosy. Sri Jagadananda himself advised him better to return to Vrindavan.

Sri Krishnachaitanyadeva learnt it and rebuked Sri Jagadananda that he should not cross his limit to advise Sri Sanatan whom Sri Chaitanyadeva himself has given shelter. Sri Chaitanyadeva with the divine touch by embracing Sri Sanatan and as a result he was cured of disease and, thereafter, stayed in Neelachal for more ten months having discussions with Sri Chaitanyadeva on various topics of Vaishnava Philosophy.

No Pain Physically or Mentally to Others

Sri Adwaitacharya once as a teacher gave advices on different topics from knowledge in order to build up Sri Gouranga's elder brother

Vishwarup. Ultimately, having studied the Scriptures and feeling inanity of family and life Vishwarup left home and took Sannyas.

Sachimaa, with the sorrow of separation with elder son was aggrieved with Sri Adwaitacharya. She felt some anger in mind towards that Adwaitacharya. While Sri Gourangadev was preparing himself in the Harinaam Sankirtan of becoming ready for this world the same Sri Adwaitacharya gave his wise company. Mother Sachidevi was afraid of Sri Adwaitacharya lest her only remaining son Nemai may leave the house for taking Sannyas.

Sri Chaitanyadeva did not spare even his mother who had enough anger to Sri Adwaitacharya in mind only. But Sri Chaitanyadeva felt it and caused her to appologise to Sri Adwaitacharya.

He used to advise all that no one should give pain physically or mentally to others even jibas of the world. "Kayamonobakyey Pranimaatre na dibe udbeg".

Due Respect to Women

Sri Chaitanyadev naturally knew very well that without women this world cannot run. Without women no one can born in this world. No one can be brought up without women. Women are as equal as Men. There should not remain any difference in Men and Women. Without women the strength of the mankind would be utilised almost half of whole amount of strength. Women should not be ignored.

So, He advised all his followers to keep respectable distances with women. There may remain relation of affection to and from mother, sister, wife, daughter and closed kith and kins.

Moreover, the women generally become more devout than men. They are highly respectable.

It is true that generally man cannot control him and so there remain chances of fall and the society becomes dirty. A Vaishnab is worshipper of God Lord Sri Krishna so he needs to remain pure in every respect. For a Vaishnav there are some rules that should be maintained by each and every devotee. Younger Haridas perhaps had crossed the boundary as he was not allowed to have any interaction with women and so for him Sri Chaitanyadeva had closed the door forever. This was a lesson for all the Bairagis and Sannyasis. Sri Chaitanyadeva always used to bow to devout women of any category.

He cautioned all from the women who could be obstacle in the path of Sadhana. Each and every man should remain pure in thoughts and deeds.

Once Sri Chaitanyadeva while was seeing at Lord Sri Sri Jagannathaswami from behind the Gadurh Pillar in ecstacy in love of Him. Tears from his eyes were falling incessantly. At that time thousands of spectators entered the Temple to have darshan of Lord Sri Sri Jagannathaswami. Among them a lady of Odisha in order to see Lord Sri Sri Jagannathaswami clearly jumped on the shoulder of Sri Chaitanyadeva. She did not care whereon she was standing. She was also in ecstacy to have darshan. To see this Sri Govinda called the lady to come down and also rebuked her. Sri Chaitanyadeva looked at her and found her eagerness to see Lord Sri Sri Jagannathaswami.

Odiya Ek Stree Virhe Darshan Na Paaiya,
Gadure Chadi Dekhe Prabhura Skandhe Paa Diya.

And

Taar Aarti Dekhi Prabhu Kahite Lagila,
Eta Aarti Jagannatha More Nahi Dila.

(Ch. Ch. By Krishnadas Kaviraj 3/14)

Sri Chaitanyadeva stopped Govinda and said that he prayed to Lord Sri Sri Jagannathaswami for having such eagerness that the lady had to see Him.

He also commented that the lady was so engrossed in Lord Sri Sri Jagannathaswami she could not care standing from where she was looking at Lord.

Jagannathe Aabista Ihar Tanu Pran Mane,
Mar Kandhe Pad Diyachhe, Taho Nahi Jaane.

(Ch. Ch. ByKrishnadas Kaviraj 3/14)

No doubt Sri Chaitanyadeva was the great.

Hard Reality and Sri Chaitanyadev

Sri Chaitanyadeva naturally was a person of hard reality. On his way from Ramkeli to Neelachal at the house of Sri Baas at Kumarhatta Sri Chaitanyadeva somehow could feel that Sri Sri Baas was running family in acute hardship because he never begged for himself. Sri Chaitanyadeva advised Ramai Pundit and other brothers including some devotees to look after this aspect so that Sri Sri Baas can maintain the family and then he would be able to think of Lord Sri Krishna without any anxiety.

Once in Sankirtan at Sribaas Angan during the songs and dances he called ordinary retailer of banana cones at corner of market Sridhar from whom he used to take banana cones gave him due respect in his team of Sankirtan.

Again he also blessed Sri Suklambar Brahmachari, an ordinary beggar by eating a handful of begged mixed rice from his bag and included him in His team of Samkirtan

Sri Basudev Dutta, a well to do person but a devotee of Sri Krishna and also of Sri Chaitanyadeva used to spend money extravagantly in many unnecessary occasions. Mahaprabhu Sri Chaitanyadeva advised another well to do devotee Sibananda Sen, who arranges to bring devotees and followers of Sri Chaitanyadeva before the Rathayatra upto Puri and their residences at Puri every year to see the matter so that Basudev cannot spend much extravagantly in each occasion. He wanted all to think where to spend and how much to afford.

Once, Banamali Pundit came to Sri Chaitanyadev to beg. He and his son were so much benefitted that they have been blessed by God Himself Sri Gouranga Mahaprabhu.

Mahaprabhu several times took the work to clean the temples at Neelachal and during His Nabadwip Lila also thinking the health aspects of thousands of devotees who gather at the sites.

Once, Sri Chaitanyadeva advised Sri Sanatan and also Subuddhi Roy to look after the followers and devotees who will reach Mathura-Vrindavan.

The Last Twelve Years of Sri Chaitanyadev

However, Sri Chaitanyadeva sent his own beloved and mostly trusted man Sri Jagadananda Pundit who was also a disciple of Sri Gadadhar Pundit to Nabadwip as a regular and annual practice to meet Sachimaa. Prasad of Lord Sri Sri Jagannathaswami for her including Srimati Vishnupriyadevi and other people of Nabadwip was arranged. After staying some more than one month he returned after meeting Sri Adwaita Acharya. Sri Adwaita Acharya gave him a letter in poetic form to hand over to Sri Chaitanyadeva. On receiving it Sri Swarup Damodar even could not apprehend the meaning. Sri Chaitanyadeva took the poem and read:-

Baulke Kahio Loke Hailo Aaaul,
Baulere Kahio Haate Na Bikay Cheul,
Baulke Kaje Nahiko Aaul,
Baulke Kahio Iha Kahiyachhe Baul.

(Ch. Ch. By Krishnadas Kaviraj 3/19)

From then Sri Chaitanyadeva remained silent. He did not like to talk with anybody else but a few closed associates and Sri Gadadhar Pundit. His condition of health was decreasing day after day but his activities seemed to be of mad.

Sri Chaitanyadeva survived only forty eight years in the world. At his twewnty four he took Sannyas. Out of the rest twenty four years almost six years have passed in touring South India, Goud Banga, Mathura-Vrindaban-Varanasi. Out of rest eighteen years he accompanying his associates passed six years and the rest twelve years he remained in Gambhira.

In these years his condition was like a mad as Srimati Radharani and other Gopis were mad to find Sri Uddhav at their Vrindaban. Whole of the days used to utter the name of Sri Krishna.

He had a regular programme to listen to the Srimad Vagawata reading by Sri Gadadhara Pundit at Tota Gopinath Temple. Sri Swarup Damodar sometime sang relating the subject of reading. Sri Chaitanyadeva and Sri Gadadhara Pundit both would weep and their tears would fall on the scripture. Sri Chaitanyadeva used to travel there by placing one hand on the shoulder of Sri Swarup Damodar or Sri Govinda. Sometime he used to fall on ditches full of water or on the bushes full of thorns.

Being mad once he jumped from the roof of Gambhira and fell on the cows. Nobody could understand even the door was duly closed and someone slept at the door how Sri Chaitanyadev could easily climbed on the roof. However, somehow he was saved by his followers.

Being mad for Lord Sri Krishna he ran towards the Chatak Hill considering the Gobardhan Hill of Gokul.

Seeing a flower garden he ran to it taking it Vrindaban the place of Lila of Lord Sri Krishna.

Being mad he wanted to jump in the sea. Once he did so considering Srimati Radharani was playing with Sri Krishna and somehow he was floating on the waves of the sea. All the associates there began to search at different directions. At last he was saved having been caught in the net of a fisherman. He with his thin and lean body like nothing but a lump of gold having no sense was rescued by Sri Swarup Damodar, Sri Govinda or Sri Shankar Pundit.

However, the last Lila in Neelachal remained mysterious to all. Even Sri Krishnadas Kaviraj remained silent in this regard. Perhaps he knew there is no end of existence of Sri Chaitanyadeva, he would be present with us all having the eternal life. He just wrote:-

Prabura Ananata Lila Na Pari Bujhite,
Buddhi-Prabesh Nahi Tate Na Pari Barnite,
Sob Shrota Vaishnavera Bandiya Charan,
Chaitanya Charit Barnan Koilo Samapan.

(Ch. Ch. By Krishnadas Kaviraj 3/20)

We do not know the reason why this old aged respectable poet avoided the fact, if any. However, according to Sri Lochandas in Sri Chaitanya Mongal has commented in his writing that in 1533 AD (1455 Shaka) in the month of Ashad on the Shukla Saptami at the third Prahar on Sunday Sri Chaitanyadeva was mixed with Sri Sri Jagannatha.

Jagannathe Leen Prabhu Haila Aapane...

(by Lochandas Ch.Mongal, Last Part, 174-178 Shloka)

Yet we find other information from the writing of Sri Vrindabandas that Sri Chaitanyadeva used to see Lord Sri Sri Jagannathadeva from behind the Gadur pillar daily. He did not touch Him. But during the nine days of Rathayatra Lord Sri Sri Jagannathadeva remained in the Gundicha Temple and there was no hard rule not to touch Him. Sri Chaitanyadeva being mad for touching Him with lifetime friend Sri Gadadhara Pundit ran towards the entrance of the Temple. It was afternoon of the same day as mentioned earlier. Being mad in love for Jagannathaswami he entered the Temple despite "No Entry" by the Padichhas on duty there.

Gadadhare Prabhu Bole - Shuna Gadadhara.
Aami Aage Jai Tumi Aasaha Pshchate.

(by Sri Vrindabandas, Ch.Bh. Antya, Chap 12,

(Published by Bulbul Bosu, Reflect Publications,30 Mahatma Gandhi Road, Kolkata 700 009, 11th December 1983 AD, Printed by Anil Dey from Union Press, 5E Ramkrishna Lane, Kolkata 700 003.)

There was no time for wasting and so Sri Gadadhara Pundit advanced towards the entrance and he also was vanished.

Eimate Mahaprabhu Gadadhar Loiya,
Nija Sthane Gela Prabhu Antardhan Hoiya.
(by Sri Vrindabandas, Ch.Bh. Antya, Chap 12,

(Published by Bulbul Bosu, Reflect Publications, 30 Mahatma Gandhi Road, Kolkata 700 009, 11th December 1983 AD, Printed by Anil Dey from Union Press, 5E Ramkrishna Lane, Kolkata 700 003.)

However, we have the belief that the spiritual consciousness of them is deathless. Still Sri Gouranga our beloved Sri Chaitanyadeva and Sri Gadadhara Pundit remain with us for their devotion to Lord Sri Krishna and sacrifice throughout their lives. So we do not observe the day of shock of their disappearances.

We should repeat that this Sri Gadadhara Pundit never became separated from his Sri Gouranga. Even at the time of last day at the Gundicha Temple in Puri Sri Gadadhara Pundit accompanied Sri Gouranga and both of them were disappeared. Thus, Sri Gadadhara Pundit kept the words of Sachimaa till his last breath. So, he was a friend indeed a friend in need. We should bow our heads to Sri Gouranga Mahaprabhu i.e. Sri Chaitanyadeva and Sri Gadadhara Pundit all the time.

Appendices

Appendix - I

Siksha Shlokastaka

Sri Gadadhara Pundit was an icon of the Shlokas. The **Siksha Shlokastaka** an octave in poetic forms composed by Sri Chaitanyadeva. There were eight Shlokas that educate a person to become pure Vaishnava.

Sri Basudev Dutta singer and composer of songs (like his brother Mukunda Dutta) once sang of the beauty of the divine couple Sri Goura-Gadadhara.

In the Shloka numbered one we find the victory of Sri Krishna Sankirtanam (Vijayatey Srikrishna Sankirtanam):-

Chetodarpana Marjanang Bhaba Mahadabagni Nirbapanang,
Shreyah Koiraba Chandrika Bitaranang Vidyabadhu Jibanam,
Anandambudhibibardhanang Pratipadang
Purnamritaswadanang
Sarbatmasnpanang Parang Vijayate Srikrishna Sankirtanam.

The process that cleanses alike the dust from the surface of a mirror a mind, that cools the heat from forest-fire of earthly life, what is for the welfare alike the way the moonlight of white lotus, that like the soul of excellently educated bride, listening to what the ocean of happiness is stirred, what is present at the step after step as the taste of nectar, what having bathed the soul in the pleasure provides complete satisfaction that Srikrishna Sankirtana be victorious.

Sri Gadadhar Pundit always maintained to observe the indication of Mahaprabhu. His love for Sri Krishna and Mahaprabhu made him so much calm and cool.

In the 2nd Shloka Mahaprabhu Sri Chaitanyadeva wrote that God has many names but lamented that he had not sufficient attachment in any of the names of Lord:-

Naamnakari Bahudha Nijashaktistatrarpita,
Etadrishi Taba Kripa
Bhagawanapi Dirdoibamidrishamhajoni
Naanuragah.

God has exposed Himself in many names and has rest all the His power on those names. So, people have the belief that the names and the owner of the names are of same important. By memorizing Him to utter regularly any of the names there remains no rule. Sri Chaitanyadeva urges - Oh, Lord, such brilliant is your kindness! Alas, it is my misfortune that I have got no attachment in thy name.

Sri Gadadhar Pundit always used to memorise or utter the name of Lord but could not be satisfied. For a real Vaishnava this dissatisfaction leads him to take God's name all the time. He also believed that God Sri Krishna of this Universe is one and He was named in many names as per the preferences in various beliefs and philosophies in different places.

Sri Chaitanyadeva has expressed in the 3rd Shloka as:-

Trinadapi Sunichena Taroriba Sahishnuna,
Amanina Manadena Kirtaniyah Sada Harih.

To become a real Vaishnava please try to be lower than a single piece of grass. Try to be tolerant like a tree what does not protest if it is cut. Give due respect to others who generally was denied any respect. Please chant the glory of the name of Lord Hari.

Sri Gadadhara Pundit was one of the accurate icon of the Shloka. To see his soft nature in interaction with others and overall behaviours of Pundit many people were attracted to him. In this connection we can remember Sri Ballav Acharya alias Sri Ballav Bhatta who was previously initiated in Sri Gopal Mantra ultimately opted initiation in adolescent Sri Krishna Yugal Mantra from him.

Sri Chaitanya Mahaprabhu has expressed in the 4th Shloka as:

Dhanang Na Janang Sundaring, Kavitang Ba Jagadisha Na Kamaye,
Moma Janmani Janmanishware Bhabatad Vaktirhoituki Twayi.

Sri Chaitanyadeva prayed to Sri Jagadisha the owner of the Universe - Oh, Lord Jagadisha I do not pray for wealth, do not expect my own men, do not wish to have beautiful wife, nor I pray for the capacity of writing poems. My only prayer is that I may get the opportunity of causeless devotion to Thy in all my births.

A *real Vaishnava* Sri Gadadhara Pundit had no personal demands for anything. He easily left all his personal and paternal wealth behind when he accompanied Sri Chaitanyadeva towards Neelachal. He did not return home. He also did not marry any woman for rendering whole heartedly service to Sri Chaitanyadeva. He did not write any poem or any article for fame although he had enough capability of writing. He wanted to serve Sri Chaitanyadeva and the diety of Gopinathji at Tota as advised by Sri Chaitanyadeva. His devotion to Lord was unmeasurable. He wanted to serve Lord in all his births.

Sri Chaitanyadeva in the 5th Shloka has expressed as:-

Oee Nandatanuja Kinkarang Patitang Maang Bhabambudhou,
Kripaya Taba Paadapankaj a Sthitadhuli Sadrishah Bichintiya.

Oh, Lord Nanda's son Sri Krishna! I am your servant fallen in the undulating ocean of mortal life. Please accept me as your servant like the smallest particle of the dust at your divine feet.

Sri Gadadhara Pundit had the conception of being a servant of Lord and throughout his life he did so accordingly.

Sri Chaitanyadeva in the 6th Shloka has expressed as:

Nayanang Galadashrudharaya Vandanang Gad Gadarudhaya Gira,
Pulakoirnichitang Bapuh Kada Taba Naamagrahney Bhabishyati.

Oh Lord, when such a day would come as my eyes would be filled with melted stream of tears while I should utter your divine name and when my mouth would be choked with the words of highly praising you with excessive emotion and my body would be thrilled with unlimited pleasure?

Pundit Sri Gadadhara always used to think as Mahaprabhu advised in the Siksha Shlokastaka an octave in poetic forms. He knew nothing more than Sri Chaitanyad Mahaprabhu.

Chaitanyadeva in the 7th Shloka has expressed as:-

Yugaitang Nimishena Chakshusha Praabrishayitam,
Shunyaitang Jagat Sarbang Govindabiharena Me.

Sri *Chaitanyadeva lamented - With the separation from Sri Govinda* a *single moment appears* to me a *longer age. My eyes have been drenched and filled with the flow of shower* as *in the rainy season and* so *the Universe seems to* me *vacant.*

Sri Gadadhara had the same feeling as Sri Chaitanyadeva wrote for real Vaishnavas. He remained as Sri Chaitanya's shadow and could feel the mind and heart of him.

Sri Chaitanyadeva in the 8th Shloka has expressed as:-

Aashlishya Sa Paadaratang Pinastu Mamadarsl1anamarmahatang Karotu Sa
Jatha Tatha Sa Biddhatu Lampato, Matprana Nathas tu Sa Eba Naaparah.

Sri Chaitanyadeva expressed in the concluding Shloka expressed that Srimati Radharani said - He is my beloved one, the only one, none else:- I am the servant at His feet and He may, if desires crush me by embracing on His chest. He may hurt me without a single stare on me. On being a polygamist may take pleasure anywhere as His choice. Yet He is my love the one, the only one, none else. Naparah...

Like Srimati Radharani of Braja had the vow only to serve Sri Krishna who having a flute in hand Sri Gadadhara Pundit also knew nothing but Lord Sri Krishna as well as Sri Gouranga Mahaprabhu i.e. Sri Chaitanyadeva. Sri Gadadhara Pundit sacrificed all the earthly materials behind including personal freedom of thinking and knew nothing but to serve from childhood to the last day on this earth. He did not hope for anything, fame, own position etc. he did not think for a moment to jump in the death trap for Sri Chaitanyadeva.

All the Vaishnavas, if desire may regard this Octave as 'Haribhakti Vilas' to become perfect Vaishnavas, lovers of Lord Sri Krishna as well as Sri Krishna Chaitanyadeva. The people of Bengal prefer to call him Sri Krishna Chaitanya Mahaprabhu or Sri Chaitanya Mahaprabhu.

Appendix - II

The Upper Genealogical Table

(Derived from Vaishnava Sahityer Sarsangraha by Kishoridas Babaji (2nd Part) and some other Kulapsnji of Kashyap Gotra)

Adisur the King brought Kashyap Gotra Brahmin in Bengal Susen Muni (Acharya, then Chaturvedi) - Brahmanya Ojha or Brahma Ojha - Daksha Shantanu - Pitambar (some says that Shantanu was son of Pitambar) - Hiranya Garva Bhugarva - Bedagarva - Jigni Mahamuni (some says that Jaganmahamuni or Jigni and Mahamuni were different persons) - Swarnarekh and Bhaba dev (Swarnarekh remained in Barendra Branch while Bhabadev went to Rarhi Branch).

Swarnarekh - Sindhu- Garurh - Kratu Bhaduri and Motu Moitra and both were declared as Kulin by the Emperor Ballal Sen) - Sankarshan Muni and Basudeva Ojha - Jogesh and Dibakar (lost Kulin stage as changed the residence) - Pundarikashya and Kubalaya Pundarikashya - Vishwambhar Acharya - Lakshmipati Acharya - Yajnik Acharya - Udayan Acharya - Pashupati (born from 2nd wife) - Ughai or Ugramuni - Kamaha - Balaha - Vilas Madhab Mishra - Jagannath or Baninath (born in Chitlagong) and Gadadhara (born in Nabadwip)

This Gadadhara did not marry but Baninath was family man.

Baninath - Nayananda and Hridayananda.

Sri Gadadhara Pundit coached the two nephews. Nayananda settled at Bharatpur. But on request of Gouridas of Kalna Hridayananda was deputed for worshipping at a temple and there he was named as Hridaya Chaitanya. Later Shyamananda became his disciple.

Appendix - II

Genealogical Table - The list of ancestors of Sri Gadadhar Pundit

It is said that from Kanauz five Brahmins were brought from King Virendra Singha of Kanauz by the then King Adisur alias Veersen of Bengal just after at the end of eleventh Century. They were Kshitish, Beetarag, Sudhanidhi, Medhatithi and Souvari of five gotras Shandilya, Kashyap, Batsya, Bhardwaz and Sabama respectively. Beetarag of Kashyap Gotra had four sons e.g. Daksha, Sushen Muni, Bhanu and Kripanidhi.

Sushen Muni (used Acharya later Chaturvedi as title)

|

Brahmanya Ojha (Brahma Ojha)

|

Daksha

|

Shantanu

|

Pitambar (some say Pitambar's son was Shantanu)

|

Hiranyagrava

|

Bhugarva

|

Vedgarva

|

Jigni Mahamuni
(Jaganmahamuni, some say Jigni and Mahamuni were separate persons)

|

Swarnarekh, (Barendra Branch) — Bhabadev (Rarhi Branch)

|

Sindhu (Sindhyaik Ojha)

|

Garhur

|

Krotu (Bhaduri), (Kratu Ketai) — Motu (Moitra) (Matu Meitai)
(The King Ballal Sen conferred honour as Kulin)

|

Sankarshan Muni, Basudev Ojha

|

Bhalluk Acharya (Daas Ojha)

|

Jogesh, — Dibakar (Lost Kaulinya for changing residence at Kargna Village)

|

Pundarikasha, Kubalaya

|

Vishwambhar Acharya

|

Lakshipati Acharya

|

Yagnrk Acharya

|

Udayayan Acharya

|

(at Baniati Village modified the Barendra Branch and written the 'Naya Kusumanjali. He had two wives. One wife gave birth to Bhupati, Bhawanipati, Chandipati, Gourpati, Rudranipati and Shachipati. They somehow lost Kaulinya.

Another wife gave birth to Pashupati who remained Kulin as father Udayan)

|

Pashupati

|

Jagai, Ghagai, Khankhair, Bankhair, Bhadai, Tarunai, Vasudev Ojha and Ughai (Ugramani)

|

Kamai, Tikai, Chamai, Subesh and Bardhaman

|

Balai, Pitai, Pushpaketan, Angshuman, Kusumsekhar, Meenketan

|

Anga, Bhanga, Vilas, Dhiman

(A certain King Chitrasen of Chittagang chose Vilas and honoured by appointing as court-poet and established him at Beleta village)

|

Sri Madahb Mishra (initiated form Sripad Madhabendrapuri in Nabadwip)

|

Jagannath (Baninath) and **Sri Gadadhar Pundit** (Unmarried)*
(bom in Chittagong) (born in Nabadwip)

|

Nayananda and Hridayananda

Sri Gadadhar Pundit brought up with proper care and education and initiated both the nephews. Later Nayananda settled at Bharatpur,

Gouridas Pundit of Kalna was in search of an honest and perfectly educated and trained young Brahmin for worshipping the Diety of Lord Sri Krishna at Kalna. On request of Gouridas Pundit Sri Gadadhar Pundit allowed Hridayananda for taking the charge of worshipping the Diety of Lord Sri Krishna at Kalna. Afterwards this Hridayananda was named 'Hridaya Chaitanya' by Sri Gouridas as he kept the Diety of Sri Chaitanya Mahaprabhu at his heart. It is known that later Sri Shyamanandaprabhu was disciple of Hridayananda.

Appendix - III

The Branch of Sri Gadadhar Pundit

Sri Gadadhar Pundit was considered as the Radha Shakti of Lord Sri Chaitanyadev at Nabadwip and Neelachal Leela as Srimati Radharani was the source of power of Lord sri Krishna at Vrindavan Leela. Sri Krishnadas Kaviraj in Sri Sri Chaitanya Charitamrita has recorded the branch of Sri Gadadhar Pundit as under: -

Sri Gadadhar Pundit Shakhate Mahattam,
Taar Upashakha Kichhu Kane Ganan.

Shakha shreshtha Dhrubananda Sridhar brahmachari,
Bhagawatacharya Haridas brahmachari.

Ananta acharya Kavi Dutta Mishra Nayan,
Ganga mantri Mamuthakur Kanthavaran.

Bhugarva Gossain aar Bhagawata Das,
Ye dui aasi koilo Vrindavane baas.

Baninath brahmachari barah mahasaya,
Ballav Chaitanyadas Krishna premmoya.

Srinath Chakraborty aar Uddhavdas,
Jita Mishra Kathkata Jagannathdas.

Sri Hari Acharya Sandipuriya Gopal,
Krishnadas brahmachari Pushpa Gopal.

Sriharsha Raghumitra Pundit Lakshminath,
Bangabati Chaitanyadas Sri Raghunath.

Chakraborty Shibananda shakhate uddaam,
Madan Gopal paayete jaar vishram.

Amogh pundit Hastigopal Chaitanya Ballav,
Jadu Ganguly aar Mongal Vaishnav.

Sangkshepe kohilo Pundit Gossainr gon,
Oichhe aar shakha upashakhar gonan.

Punditer gon sob Bhagawata ddhanya,
Pranballav sobar Srikrishnachaitanya, (Original in Bengali, Ch.Ch.Adi 12 p.)

Appendix - IV

Sri Sri Gadadharastakam

Swabhaktiyoga Laasinang Sadabraje Biharinang
Haripriya Ganagragang Sachisuta-Pryeswarang.
SaRadha Krishnasebana Prakashakang Mahasayang
Vajamyahang Gadadharang Supanditang Gurung Prabhum..(1)

Nabojjwaladi Bhabna Bidhan Karma Paragang
Vichitra Gourabhakti Sindhu Ranga Bhanga Laasinang.
Surag Marga Darshakang Brajadibaasa Dayakang
Vajamyahang Gadadharang Supanditang Gurung Prabhum..(2)

Sachi Sutanghrisara Bhaktavrinda-Bandya Gourabat
Gourabhav Chittapadma Madhya Krishna Suballabhang.
Mukunda Goura Roopinang Swa-Bhav-Dharma Dayakang
Vajamyahang Gadadharang Supanditang Gurung Prabhum..(3)

Nikunja -Sbanadika-Prakashnoika-Swaroopakang
Sada Sakhiriti Pradang Maharasa Swaroopakang
Sadashritanghri-Pundari-pradang Sad Gurungbarang
Vajamyahang Gadadharang Supanditang Gurung Prabhum..(4)

Mahaprabho MaharasoPrakashanamkurang Priyang
Sada Maharasoamkura Prakashanadi-Basanag.
Mahaprabho vrajanganadi Bhav-Moda-Karakang
Vajamyahang Gadadharang Supanditang Gurung Prabhum..(5)

Dwijendra-Vrinda-Bandya-Paadyugma Bhakti Bardhakang
Nijeshu Radhikatmata-Bopuh Prakahsanagraham.
Ashesh Bhakti Shashtra Shikshyojjwalamrita-Pradang
Vajamyahang Gadadharang Supanditang Gurung Prabhum..(6)

Muda-Nija-Priyadika-SwaPadapdma Sidhuvir
Maharosomabamrita-Pradesta-Goura-Bhaktika-Dayakang,
Sadasta Swatwikanitang Nijesta-Bhakti dayakang
Vajamyahang Gadadharang Supanditang Gurung Prabhum..(7)

Yadtya Reetiraraaga-Rangabhanga-Oigdha Manaso,
Narehpi Yati Turnameba Naryabhava-Bhajanang.
Tamujjwalakata-Chittameba Chitta Matta-Shat Pado,
Vajamyahang Gadadharang Supanditang Gurung Prabhum..(8)

Maharasamrita-Pradang Sada Gadadharastakang,
Pathettu Yah Subhaktito Brajangana-Ganotsabam.
Sachitanuja-Paadpadma-Bhaktiratna-Yogyatang,
Labheta Radhika Gadadharngghri-Padmasebaya.

Eti Srila Swaroop Goswamivirachitang Sri Sri Gadadharastakam Samaptam.

Appendix - V

Sadhak Mukundalal Goswamt believed -

Revered readers may please also note that Anantasri Sadhak Mukundalal Goswami believed in Yugal worshipping of Sri Sri Radhakrishna as well as Sri Sri Gour-Gadadhara. Keeping in belief that Sri Radha is Sri Gadadhar Pundit in the Kaliyuga he used to collect hundreds of the views to establish his views in the middle of the last Century. Some of them are as under: -

(i) Lokenath Goswami had written in his Gadadharastakam - 'Mahabhav - Swararupakang Twang Bande Radhikabhidhang\ (he collected from Oriental Library, Madras),

(ii) In Chaitanyarchan Chandrika - 'Baame Gadadharadevang Hladinishakti Vigraham',

(iii) Brahma Haridas wrote - 'Bhanusuta Avatara Gadai Pundit',

(iv) In Nabadwip Yogapeeth description - 'Madhye Goura Krishneswara, Dakshine Netai Haladhara Baame Gadadhara Radharoop'

(v) In one Panchatattwa prayer:-

Praseeda Sri Nabadwip, Sri Gange Sri Guro Hare,

Sri Gourangaprabho, Nityanandadwaita Kripamaba!

Hey Gadadhar! Sachisuta Haarddapatra! Gaandharbika Sukhatano,

Rasargaatra! Maangte Padabjarajasa Sadrikang Bibhavya

Kirting Pracharaya Neejang Kushaloirbibhavya,

Bhataa Gourahareh Parangmoyee Kripang Kurbantu Naanyagatoi.

(vi) In another Prayer:-

.... Ratnabatinandana Premapatra Haa Nath Madhabacharyaputra.

Sri Gouranga Premarasa Vilasa Haa Gadadhar Kurutehnghri Dasa.

(vii) Narottam Thakur expressed - "Gadadhar Mor Kool",

(viii) Radharamandas in his prayer said- "Hey Gadadhar Seva Diye Karo Angikar",

(ix) In one Kirtan after return-

"Gour Elore Gharey Gour Elo Gharey,
Gadadharer Haath Dhari Brabhamanye Koirey.
Gour Elo Gadai Elo Aar Elo Netai,
Elo Aar Yata Bhaktaloye Adwait Gossain."

(x) In another Kirtan - 'Gadahar Vilas Sindhu'."

Index

A

Aatharonala, 101
Abadwip Sri Nemai, 28
Actual identity, 104
Adhyapak Shiromani, 28
Adiguru Shankaracharya, 108
Adwaita Acharya, 151
Agarpara, 121
An Intruder Brahmin, 72
Aniseed powder mixed, 123
Arail Village, 138
Arail Village near Prayag, 143, 145
Ariadah, 122
Astrology, 26
Atish Dipankar, 38

B

Baby Krishna, 56
Balabhadra Bhattacharya, 137
Ballav Bhatta, 143
Banana, 148
Banana cones, 158
Bank of the Ganga, 120
Bardhaman district, 73
Basudev Dutta, 73
Bay of Bengal, 92, 106
Bearer of the name, 17
Belghoria, 122
Belur, 108
Bengali Year, 31
Betal Pargana, 38
Betel leafs, 24
Betel leaves, 55, 71
Bhagabat Purana, 145
Bhagavadgita, 145
Bhagirathi, 70
Bhramar Gita, 99
Big laddus of different rice made chida, 123
Bijuli Khan, 138
Bindu Sarobar, 100
Black pepper powder, 123
Boarder guards, 96
Boarding facilities, 68
Bolgandi, 123
Brahma-sutra, 145
Brahmagiri, 108
Brahmin, 79
Brahmin family, 29
Brahmin traveller, 20
Brahmin-curse as a Boon, 72
Braja, 99
Braja Dham, 138
Braja or Vrindaban, 24
Brajendra-Nanadan, 86
Burhan village, 52

C

Calves of the cows, 84
Chaitanya Mahaprabhu, 141
Champaran (Raipur), 143
Chand Kazi, 81
Chandi Mandap, 44
Chandipur, 108
Chida, 148

Chilka Lake, 107
Coconut laddu, 123
Coconut pieces, 123
Colourful flags, 125
Condensed milk, 123
Curd, 148
Cuttack, 100, 117

D

Dabir Khas, 120
Dakshina Mathura, 107
Decorated elephants, 115
Deers, 135
Denur village, 73
Devghar, 108
Dhaka Dakshin, 38
Dhanutirtha, 108
District of Dhaka, 38
Divine Life Sketch, 124
Divine Lilas, 130
Divine look, 116
Divine pleasure, 71
Divine weapon Sudarshan, 123
Dohad, 108
Dr. Sarvapalli Radhakrishnan, 145
Drama Rukmini Sambad, 33
Dried jujube, 123

E

Early stage, 16
East Bengal, 38, 135
Eastern side of the sea, 107
Education in the society, 17
Elder brother Vishwarup, 107
Elephants, 135
Elephants and horses, 33

F

Family life after marriage, 121
Famous teacher in Nabadwip town, 25
Faridpur, 38
Father Nanda, 99
Feast for the Vaishnavas, 28
Female character, 69
Female demon, 56
Female singer, 113
Flower garden, 130
Fortunate devotee, 44
Fortunate people, 80
Fried chida, 123

G

Gadadhara Pundit, 53
Gadurh Pillar, 105
Ganga, 70, 114, 135
Garlands of fragrant flowers, 24
Gaud Bengal, 133, 151
Gaud to Mathura-Vrindaban, 120
'Ghat' of the Ganga, 27
Ghats of the Ganga, 19
Ginger with lemon juice, 123
Ginger with mustard oil paste, 123
Gobardhan Hill of Gokul, 159
Godavari, 108
Goddess of learning, 34
Goddess of strength, 70
Gokarna, 108
Golden jwelleries, 21
Golden ornaments, 20
Gopa mantra, 144
Gopinath remains, 98
Goud Bengal, 97, 111, 115, 125, 131, 146
Goud Lila, 127
Grammar for children, 36
Great surprise, 99
Great zaminder, 95
Gundicha Temple, 32, 123, 124, 126
Gunja Mala, 150
Guruvayur - Shringeri Mutt, 108

H

Hanuman Ghat, 143

Hara-Gouri, 40
Harinaam Movement, 16, 91
Harinaam Sankirtan, 47, 72, 117, 121, 143
Harinaam Sankirtan Jajna, 87
Harinaam Sankirtan Mahajajna, 71
Harinaam Sankirtan Mahayajna, 48, 52, 59
Hazipur, 141
Hindolika Vihar, 23
His Lilas with the Braja Gopis, 92
His Nabadwip Lila, 158
Historical debate, 36
Hooghly, 122, 123
Hussein Shah, 140
Hussein Shah of Goud, 96

J

Jagai and Madhai, 61
Jagannath Mishra, 21
Jagannath Pur, 107
Jagannatha Mishra, 20
Jagat Janani, 90
Jajpur, 100
Jay Jagannath, 125
Jayananda, 33
Jewels studded anklets, 51
Jharikhanda, 143
Jinda Peer, 147
Jujube, 123
Jujube powder, 123

K

Kaladi village, 108
Kali-Durga-Yogamaya, 70
Kalinga area, 96
Kamala-Hari, 40
Kamalpur, 101
Kanyakumari, 107, 108
Karnataka State, 25
Kashidham, 100, 143
Keshav Bharati, 90
Keshav Kashmiri Pundit, 34
Khardah, 122
Killed Kansa of Mathura, 77
King Kansa, 56, 57
King of Braja, 86
King Pratap Rudra, 127, 128
King Shishupal, 67
Kirtan with their Mridanga, 96
Kolhapur, 108
Kolkata proper, 64
Konnagar, 122
Kotwal Hussein Shah, 120
Krishna lilamrita, 41
Krishnadas Babaji, 33
Krishnadas Kaviraj, 33
Kulin Gram, 126
Kumarhatta, 121, 122
Kumarhatta (Halisahar), 118
Kusheshwar Shiva, 101

L

Laddu of coriander, 123
Laddu of rice fried in ghee, 123
Lake of Kalidah, 137
Laxmikaachh, 67
Laxmipriya Devi, 26, 28
Lila in Neelachal, 160
Liquid mustard oil paste, 123
Lochandas, 33
Longer hardship, 26
Lord Brahma, 60
Lord Jagannath, 151
Lord Jagannathaswami, 131
Lord Nemai, 32
Lord Shiva Mahadeva, 69
Lord Shiva or Bhaba, 36
Lord Sri Gopal, 76
Lord Sri Krishna, 43, 48, 52, 136, 150, 158

Lord Vishnu, 77
Love without enemity, 15
Love-affection, 17
Lovely younger brother, 19

M

Madia Panji (Panjika), 124
Mahabharata, 96
Mahaprabhu travelled to Nabadwip, 87
Mahattang Gangayah, 36
Mahendra Hills, 107
Malaya Hills, 108
Malini Devi, 85
Mango, 148
Mango pickled and sauces, 123
Mango pieces, 123
Mangopaste, 123
Masir Bari, 123
Mass movement, 84
Maternal uncle, 82
Mathura, 46, 92, 99
Mathura-Vrindaban, 115, 131, 135, 136, 137, 143, 144
Mathura-Vrindaban tour, 122
Mathura-Vrindaban-Varanasi, 159
Mega Ratha Yatra, 151
Meghamali, 21
Monikornica Ghat, 135
Mother Jashoda, 99
Mother Sachidevi, 21, 90
Mother Shaktidevi, 100
Mother-in-law of Sribaas, 72
Mudki, 123
Murari Gupta, 29, 76
Murshidabad, 79
Musical instruments, 80
Muslim family, 52
Mutt in Puri, 153

N

Nabadwip, 29, 49, 64, 71, 79, 80, 153
Nabadwip area, 71
Nabadwip Leela, 113
Nabadwip Lila, 30
Nabadwip of Bengal, 53
Nabadwip town, 21
Nadia district, 52
Nalanda Mahavihar, 38
Naodapara, 122
Narayani a Female Child, 72
Narendra Sarobar, 143
Narmada River, 108
Natagarh, 121
Naughtiness, 19
Neelachal, 105, 113, 117, 123, 132, 147, 148, 153
Neelachal Leela, 103, 113
Neelachal or Mathura-Vrindaban, 116
Neelachal, 139
Nemai Pundit, 30, 34
New student, 104
Nityananda Prabhu, 53
Non-Brahmin Kayaystha, 146

O

Oiled mango, 123
Old powder of bitter leaves, 123
Omkareswar, Ujjain, 108

P

Palatable dishes, 20, 93
Panchapsara-Yog Falls, 108
Panchvati, 108
Pandharpur, 108
Pandyasthan, 108
Panihati, 118, 122, 123
Peace-loving people, 79
Philosophical treatise, 26
Philosophy from Sri Sudarshan Pundit, 26
Philosophy of Vaishnava Culture, 33
Pleasant breeze, 34

Pottakodal, 108
Prayag Ghat, 96
Preceptor Keshab Bharati, 92
Preferable bridegroom, 26
Pundit Jagannath Mishra, 34
Purandar Pundit, 26
Puri (Neelachal), 104
Puri Kamkosthi, 107
Puri towards the eastern coast, 106
Puri-Neelachal, 111

R

Radha Kunda, 150
Radha Madana Gopal, 94
Radhakrishna Yugal Mantra, 59
Radharani of Braja, 154
Raipur, 108
Raja Laxman Sen of Bengal, 100
Raja Pratap Rudra, 96
Rajput Krishnadas, 138
Rama-Sita, 40
Ramai Pundit, 157
Ratha Yatra, 153
Rathayatra, 123, 131
Rathayatra of Lord Jagannathaswami, 131
Ratnadevi, 59
Real human, 17
Respect to seniors, 17
Rich fragrant spices, 55
River Ganga, 35, 115, 117
Royal Bengal Tiger, 96
Rukmini Sambad, 67, 71

S

Sachidevi, 22
Sachimaa, 20
Sagir Mullick, 120
Sahyadri Hills, 108
Sakhis, 99
Sanctum of the temple, 103
Sandal wood paste, 115
Sankirtan, 79, 82, 99, 106, 125
Sankirtan Mahajajna, 86
Sankirtan of Harinaam, 50
Sannyas Mantra, 93
Sannyasi, 18
Sanskrit Grammar, 34
Sanskrit literature, 67
Sapta Godavari, 108
Satyabhanu Upadhaya, 20
Shankaranya, 18
Shantipur, 126
Shibaninagar, 108
Shiva Mahadeva, 26, 83, 96, 100
Shyam Kunda, 150
Simple seller of banana leaves, 25
Singing and dancing, 84
Sita-Ram, 27
Skhchar, 121
Small and big factories, 17
Smriti (Law), 26
Sodepur, 121
Sorrow of separation, 156
Sri Adwaita Acharya, 26, 31, 48, 49, 52, 60
Sri Adwaita Prabhu, 27
Sri Balabhadra Bhattacharya, 136
Sri Ballavacharya Mishra, 26
Sri Banamali Acharya, 27
Sri Bhugarva, 39
Sri Chaitanyadeva, 127
Sri Chandrasekhar, 37
Sri Chandrasekhar Acharya, 27
Sri Gadadhar Pundit, 27, 29
Sri Gadadhara, 27
Sri Gopal Bhatta, 39
Sri Jadunandan Acharya, 148
Sri Jagannatha Mishra, 26
Sri Keshav Kashmiri, 37
Sri Keshav Kashmiri Pundit, 35, 36

Sri Krishna Mantra, 42
Sri Krishnadas Kaviraj, 39
Sri Lakshmipriya Devi, 26
Sri Lokenath, 39
Sri Madbhagawata Mahapuran Putana, 56
Sri Madhab Mishra, 27, 59
Sri Malini Devi, 27
Sri Mukunda, 37
Sri Murari, 37
Sri Murari Gupta, 30
Sri Nemai, 30
Sri Nilambar Chakraborty, 45
Sri Nityananda, 127
Sri Pada of Lord Vishnu, 42
Sri Ratnabati Devi, 27
Sri Ratnagarva Pundit, 44
Sri Roop Goswami, 33
Sri Shibananda Sen, 133
Sri Shuklambar Brahamachari, 94
Sri Sita Devi, 27
Sri Sri Baas Pundit, 27
Sri Sribaas, 37
Sri Sribaas Pundit, 27
Sri Subuddhi Roy, 39
Sri Swarup Damodar, 149
Sri Uddhab, 46
Sri Vijay Das, 76
Sri Vishnu Mishra, 26
Sribaas Angan, 65, 71
Srihatta (Sylhet), 38
Srimad Bhagawata, 44
Srimati Laxmipriya devi, 28, 39
Srimati Parvati, 69
Srimati Radharani, 43, 69, 70, 85, 92, 159
Srimati Radharani in Braja, 45
Srimati Shreedevi, 93
Srimati Sitadevi, 69, 93, 151
Sripad Ishwarpuri, 41, 42
Sripad Madhabendrapuri, 41
Subarna Village, 38
Suklambar Brahmachari, 42, 43
Sultan Hussein Shah, 79, 81, 82, 120
Sultanate forces, 71
Supernatural powers, 19
Surparak, 108
Sylhet, 38
Sylhet origin, 21

T

Tapti River, 108
Tax collector, 96, 97
Teachings by Lifestyle, 154
Temple area, 96
Temples of Shiva, 100
The Ganga, 121
Thiruvattur, 108
Tigers, 135
Tota Gopinath Temple, 159
Trambakeswar, 108
Twelve spots of the body, 68

U

Uddhaba, 99
Uncultured behave, 17
Union Press, 160, 161
Unparalleled scholar, 23
Unwillingness of marriage, 40
Upanishadas, 145
Upper-class people, 79
Uththan Dwadashi, 131, 133

V

Vaishnava Abhidhan, 19
Vaishnava Philosophy, 155
Vaishnava Scriptures, 39
Vaishnavas from Bengal, 149
Vaishnavism, 41, 139
Valuable ornaments, 21
Varanasi, 39, 140

Various deities, 100
Varshana village of Braja, 70
Vedanta-Upanishads, 141
Vedantik Prakashananda Saraswati, 141
Veg chida, 123
Vellimalai, 108
Victory of Nemai Pundit, 37
Vidyanagar, 108
Vijaya Dashami, 115
Vikrampore Panchasar, 38
Village Chouda, 116
Village Gobardhan, 136
Village Sukhchar, 123
Vishnupriyadevi, 47, 63, 88
Vishnusawmin, 145
Vishwaroop, 21, 22
Vrindaban, 23, 46, 92, 135, 137, 139
Vrindaban Lila, 77, 127
Vrindaban via Goud Bengal, 114
Vrindabandas, 33, 72

W

Water of the Ganga, 123
Water of the Yamuna, 93

Y

Yaban Haridas, 52
Yaban Ruler, 147
Yamuna, 93
Yawan Ruler, 117
Yoti in Varanasi, 143
Young ascetic, 103
Younger Haridas, 156
Yudhisthira, 96

Z

Zaminder of Nabadwip, 61